THE MAGADDINO-TODARO MAFIA
CRIME FAMILY

The Complete History Of The Buffalo Criminal Organization

MAFIA LIBRARY

© **Copyright 2024 - All rights reserved.**

The content contained within this book may not be reproduced, duplicated or transmitted without direct written permission from the author or the publisher.

Under no circumstances will any blame or legal responsibility be held against the publisher, or author, for any damages, reparation, or monetary loss due to the information contained within this book, either directly or indirectly.

Legal Notice:

This book is copyright protected. It is only for personal use. You cannot amend, distribute, sell, use, quote or paraphrase any part, or the content within this book, without the consent of the author or publisher.

Disclaimer Notice:

Please note the information contained within this document is for educational and entertainment purposes only. All effort has been executed to present accurate, up to date, reliable, complete information. No warranties of any kind are declared or implied. Readers acknowledge that the author is not engaged in the rendering of legal, financial, medical or professional advice. The content within this book has been derived from various sources. Please consult a licensed professional before attempting any techniques outlined in this book.

By reading this document, the reader agrees that under no circumstances is the author responsible for any losses, direct or indirect, that are incurred as a result of the use of the information contained within this document, including, but not limited to, errors, omissions, or inaccuracies.

TABLE OF CONTENTS

Introduction 1

Part I : The Dicarlo-Palmeri Era (1910-1922) 5

  Chapter 1 : The Palmeri And Dicarlo Years 7

    An Unlikely Pairing 8

      Angelo Palmeri 9

      Giuseppe Dicarlo 10

      The Start Of The Buffalo Crime Family 13

    The Years Of Success 14

    The Decline 16

    The Palmeri-Dicarlo Legacy 18

Part II : The Magaddino Era (1922-1980s) 21

  Chapter 2 : The Early Years Of Stefano Magaddino 23

    The Good Killers' Case 25

      The Murder Of Pietro Magaddino 25

      Stefano's Vengeance 27

      The Sting And The Trial 28

    Becoming The Undertaker 30

  Chapter 3 : The Reign Of The Magaddino Crime Family 33

    Expansion And Power Plays 34

Bootlegging Gold 36
  The 18th Amendment.. 36
  Magaddino's Role In The Alcohol Racket 37
Castellammarese War And The Commission 38
  The Landscape Of The War 39
  Aftermath And The Commission 41
Triumphs And Setbacks.. 42

Chapter 4 : The Magaddino Family After Prohibition 45

The End Of Prohibition 45
The Impact Of The Magaddino Family 47
  The Apalachin Meeting 49
The Sign Of Descent 51

Chapter 5 : Internal Strife, Decline, And The Power Vacuum
.... 55

Internal Conflicts And Power Struggles 56
Attempts On Stefano Magaddino's Life 57
  1936 Attempt.. 58
  After Apalachin And The 1958 Attempt 59
The Rise In Drug Trafficking And The Heroin Trade 61
Law Enforcement Efforts 62
Loss Of Influence And Territory... 63
The Final Years Of The Magaddino Family 64
The Power Vacuum And Power Struggles 68

Part III : The Todaro Family (1980s-2020s-Present) 69

Chapter 6 : The State Of The Mafia In The 1980s 71

    The Changing Landscape Of Organized Crime 72

    Increased Law Enforcement Efforts 74

    The Changing Dynamics Within The Mafia 76

    The Impact Of Public Perception And Media 78

    A New Leader On The Rise 80

Chapter 7 : Joseph "Papa Joe" Todaro Sr. 81

    The Early Years Of Todaro 82

    From Caporegime To Boss 85

        1984-1990 85

        The 1990s 89

    The Final Years Of Papa Joe Todaro 92

Chapter 8 : Joseph "Big Joe" Todaro Jr. 95

    The Early Years 96

    The Buffalo Crime Family And The 1990s 98

    Todaro Sr.'S Retirement And Rumors 100

        The Canadian Connection 102

    Current Standings Of The Todaro Family 106

Chapter 9 : The Current Regime And The Future Of Organized Crime 109

    Administrators 109

        Boss: Joseph A. "Big Joe" Todaro Jr. 109

        Underboss: Domenico "Dom" Violi 110

  Consigliere: Unknown 111

 Caporegimes 112
  Buffalo Faction 112
  Canadian Faction 112

 Soldiers 113
  Buffalo Faction 113
  Canadian Faction 115

 Associates 115
  Buffalo Faction 115
  Utica Faction 118

 Allied Groups 120
  Buffalo Chapter Of The Outlaws 120
  Niagara Chapter Of The Hells Angels (Canada) 120

 The Future Of Organized Crime And The Buffalo Crime Family 121
  Future Activities 122
  Law Enforcement Crackdown 123
  The Buffalo Crime Family 124

Conclusion 127

References 129

INTRODUCTION

In the history books of American organized crime, certain names echo with a particular resonance that makes them hard to forget. We've long been familiar with the Chicago Outfit, the Five Families based in New York, and the Philadelphia Mob. These organizations define the very thing that comes to mind when we think about the criminal underworld. Their stories have been told, retold, and reimagined in countless articles, books, movies, and TV shows, cementing their place in our memories and intertwining them with the very fabric of American organized crime.

However, amid these larger-than-life figures and notorious syndicates, the story of the Buffalo Crime Family has been often overlooked. It's not because their story lacks intrigue or significance. That's far from the truth because the saga of the Buffalo Crime Family is just as compelling as their more famous counterparts. While seemingly hanging on to obscurity, the family actually has always flown just far enough beneath the radar. Maybe they knew how to deflect attention from themselves or maybe all the credit lies with their geographical location. But they had just as much impact as their counterparts on their regions, the United States and Canada, and the Mafia as a whole.

In this book, we are looking at more than a "Golden Age" of a particular outfit. We're going to pull the Buffalo Crime Family out of their shadows and into a new light. It's a journey that takes us through the earliest days when it was trying to take hold in a growing country. It will trace the evolution from the DiCarlo-Palmeri Family and the Magaddino Family to the present-day Todaro Family. That evolution makes this organization one of the most powerful Mafia establishments in the United States. Their story is about power, ambition, betrayal, resilience, and all of it playing against an ever-changing backdrop of US history.

This narrative will start with Angelo Palmeri, who really is the founding father of this branch of the American Mafia. His beginnings, rising up through the ranks across the American landscape to establish an empire that has lasted over a century, echo that of many mafiosos. While his reign didn't speak much of notoriety, his work set the new era of the American Mafia in motion and the stage for the rise of some of the most powerful mobsters.

Palmeri's reign was short, and it was short for a good reason. He was a powerful force, but he lacked direction and a real vision for the future of an empire. So, he passed down the reigns to Giuseppe DiCarlo and took his place as underboss. Under this formidable due, the Buffalo Crime Family would expand its operations, planting roots far beyond the city of Buffalo. Now known as the DiCarlo-Palmeri family, their era was characterized by a ruthless sense of efficiency and a hunger for even more power. This was one of the strongest beginnings of a criminal outfit. They asserted their dominance and left a secure foundation to build on.

However, the DiCarlo-Palmeri reign did not last for very long. DiCarlo was already an aged man, and this meant that a new leader would need to come in and continue to push the family forward into a new regime. Enter Stefano Magaddino. Under Stefano's reign, the Buffalo Crime Family, now infamously known as the Magaddino Crime Family, would find a long period of success and influence. Stefano was a man who had immense charisma and ruthless ambition. Magaddino would further expand the Buffalo region and take the family to heights of power that were unheard of at the time. He, and the family, were a force to be reckoned with in the Mafia landscape.

But all empires reach their end, one way or another. There were already whispers of dissent during his last days, and the death of Stefano Magaddino would not just mark the end of a long era of the Buffalo family, it would also throw the entire organization into disarray. While leaders were still in place, leadership was more about holding the family's operations together. However, rising up through the ranks years before Magaddino's death was a leader who could retake control. Joseph Todaro Sr. would rebrand the Buffalo Crime Family into the Todaro family. "Papa Joe," as he was known, was someone with the vision, determination, and resilience that the family needed. He would take control of the family and help them grow from a traditional Mafia family into a modern enterprise of the criminal underworld.

As such, the Todaro Era took a huge detour from the ways of the old guard and put them onto a path that Joseph "Big Joe" Todaro Jr. is still trying to navigate today. The family now has expanded more into legitimate businesses and taken advantage of the opportunities set out by the modern world. However, no matter the landscape, the Todaro family never strays too far from the roots that are in place. The Buffalo Crime family is one that values loyalty, respect, and honor. While those are pieces of every Mafia family, they are the components that have kept the Buffalo Crime family thriving no matter what challenges are placed before them.

This book will be more than just a chronicle of the constant rise and fall of their criminal empire. Instead, it will be more of a window into a world that rarely comes into the public eye. The Buffalo family is one that exists in the shadows, controlled by its own set of rules and codes. This book is a journey into this specific part of the American underworld, giving you a glimpse at the men who ran it and the events that defined it. From the humble beginnings of the DiCarlo-Palmeri Family to the modern-day enterprise of the Todaro Family, this is the story of the Buffalo Crime Family.

And as you delve into the pages here, you'll find yourself face-to-face with the men who built this empire and a few other figures of the criminal underworld. This is a reminder that every piece of the American Mafia is connected, and one person's story easily blends into another's. Therefore, if you need to, take some time and connect the dots. Watch as you move the pieces around again and again as you try to establish the entire timeline of the Mafia. It truly is fascinating and endlessly intriguing to watch as their world unfolds parallel to ours, almost like a separate, grittier world hiding in plain sight.

So, prepare for a deep dive into a dark spot in the history of Buffalo, New York with the Buffalo Crime Family.

PART I
THE DICARLO-PALMERI ERA
(1910-1922)

CHAPTER 1
THE PALMERI AND DICARLO YEARS

Buffalo, New York boomed with an infectious energy as the US moved into the 20th century. Factories seemed to spring up overnight, industries roared, and opportunity hung heavy in the air. The Erie Canal solidified that opportunity when the watery ribbon sliced through the state in 1825. Buffalo was now a bustling transport hub. This was attractive to many immigrants, as they looked for a better life. They placed their hopes and dreams into the city, looking to have a more peaceful life than what was being offered in New York City.

But that prosperity would come with its own problems and let a darker side in. The city's growth took place at such a rapid rate that social services were spread thin and law enforcement struggled to keep up. This lack of authority opened up the floodgates for criminal activity. Gangs sprouted like weeds, all trying to stake their claim in the growing city. They tried to replicate the movement that was happening in other parts of the country and establish their own empires. Various rackets popped up, with little pushback, but there was a glaring omission from this criminal world: An empire.

This wasn't a unique occurrence, and the back-and-forth dance between ambition and illegal activity was playing out the same way in many growing American cities. However, things were about to change in a very interesting way. The Buffalo Crime Family was a soon-to-be well-oiled machine in the criminal underworld, but it would be a machine built on chance. Being in the right place at the right time would ring particularly true with the unlikely partnership between Benedetto Angelo "Buffalo Bill" Palmeri and Giuseppe DiCarlo.

Palmeri was a Sicilian firebrand with a short fuse and a penchant for violence. He was volatile, which made him feared, but he wasn't boss material. DiCarlo, however, was the embodiment of cool and calculated. He was a strategist who could map a criminal empire as if it were a game of chess. The two men, despite being as different as night and day, were put together by fate. They would form an alliance that set the stage for an operation that still continues today.

But while their legacy would be cemented, their chapter of the story was brief. However, given the era that it was, their personalities and ambition proved to be a force that made the Buffalo Crime Family.

An Unlikely Pairing

The story of the Buffalo Crime Family's rise to power would have never existed without the chance meeting and partnership of two men. Angelo Palmeri and Giuseppe DiCarlo would have vastly different backgrounds and vastly different methods for handling their business. However, when they came together, the stage was set to make the northwestern region of New York one of the most important hubs for Mafia activity.

Angelo Palmeri

Angelo Palmeri, who would establish the Sicilian hold in Buffalo and become the feared figure in the early years of the Buffalo family, wasn't born immersed in the world of petty crime and power struggles. This was vastly different from his contemporaries who rose through the ranks of organized crime, as he found his life to be one of relative comfort.

Angelo was born in January 1878 to Anna and Francesco Palmeri. Francesco was a relatively successful merchant in Castellammare del Golfo, Sicily, and Angelo was able to enjoy the rewards of his father's hard work. There was no story of clawing up from poverty or "humble beginnings" for Angelo.

Despite the comfort of his upbringing, there was a restlessness growing within the young Palmeri. In 1906, with his sights set on something more thrilling, he made a decision that forever changed the landscape of Buffalo. Leaving behind the life of comfort in Sicily, Angelo made his way across the Atlantic toward new horizons. New York City, which was the lively gateway into America for immigrants, was where he first set foot. Here, the son of a Sicilian merchant found himself lost in the reality that was working-class life. Angelo quickly found work on the docks, biding his time while planning his next move.

Six years later, in 1912, Angelo would move farther west. He would plant his roots in the northwest region of New York in Buffalo, a city that was growing, which meant that there were opportunities to take hold of its underbelly. It was here that he took his own steps into the world of business, which would start the dramatic shift in his life and the city's history. He opened a tavern on Dante Place, a seemingly normal establishment where locals could have drinks and share a laugh. However, like most of these ventures, there was so much more behind the "innocent" facade. The tavern on Dante Place was a front for gambling operations.

This venture into the criminal underworld was Angelo putting his feet to the fire. The web of illegal gambling was a risky venture that was constantly catching the attention of local authorities. While this established the future Buffalo family, Angelo's luck would run out in the same year that the tavern was opened. In a meticulously planned raid, Buffalo police targeted the growing gambling scene in the city. Angelo, along with ten other proprietors, were all arrested and convicted. This brush with the law resulted in the young Palmeri paying a fine of $50. It was a setback, but this wouldn't deter the man who was, for all intents and purposes, the founder of the Buffalo Crime Family.

This incident, while minor, exposed a very crucial flaw in Angelo's approach. Palmeri had the fire and ambition to succeed, and while he found minor success, his volatile nature would leave him without any real direction. He needed a guiding force, someone who could manage his impulsiveness while channeling his drive into something more. Angelo's missing piece was there, and once he found it, it would set the pieces in motion to create the silent, yet powerful Buffalo Crime Family.

Giuseppe DiCarlo

Born on October 18, 1873, in the town of Vallelunga, Giuseppe DiCarlo's upbringing stood in contrast to the more privileged existence of Angelo Palmeri. His parents, Francesco and Giuseppa Spera DiCarlo, were working-class people, which meant they were laboring tirelessly to make ends meet and provide for the family. Their humble surroundings and their struggle for survival were all aspects of life shared by those in the criminal underworld. Like many who would become part of the Mafia, Giuseppe's resolve was established by this humble upbringing. It instilled a burning desire to go beyond the life that he knew.

In 1905, Giuseppe took a chance to chase that fortune across the Atlantic Ocean and in the bustling heart of New York City. There, amidst the noise and dizzying pace of life, Giuseppe found his first venture with Salvatore Manzella, a fellow immigrant who was a long-standing produce merchant. Their partnership proved to be more than just a business arrangement; it was one where Giuseppe would learn everything he would need to know. While Giuseppe's time here was brief, his eye wasn't on just being a successful merchant. He wanted more than that; he wanted the American dream.

A year after DiCarlo arrived in the United States, his wife and children, including his son Joseph DiCarlo (who would go on to be a prominent member of the Buffalo Crime Family long after his father's death), joined him in New York. The DiCarlo family didn't find immediate footing in their new home. They moved around a few times, from the busy streets of Brooklyn to the vibrant blend of people in East Harlem. They would eventually settle down in 1908 in Buffalo, the city known for its industrial growth and diverse population. This is when Giuseppe would start to establish himself as a figure in the history of the region.

In 1909, Giuseppe DiCarlo along with Pietro Manzella and Carmelo Cugino established the Buffalo Italian Importing Company. This would be a tremendous step forward, especially for DiCarlo, given his life growing up. This venture would represent all three men's desire to establish their hold on the growing landscape of American Business.

The Buffalo Italian Importing Company's primary focus was going to be on the import and distribution of Italian goods. The business model was aimed at the growing Italian-American community in the region. It would let them chase their own aspirations while being able to have a bit of home there with them. The imports were innocent enough, from olive oil and pasta to wines and cheeses. However, things didn't go very smoothly for the import company.

Not long after the Buffalo Italian Importing Company was founded, there were accusations of fraudulent business practices surfacing. These allegations were heavy for an upstart company, damaging its reputation and slowing operations. There were claims stating that they were involved in unethical activities, which included misrepresenting their finances and engaging in unfair trade practices. A huge shadow was cast upon the business, and the men lost the trust of their clients and trading partners.

The allegations would continue to pile on and the legal scrutiny that followed put tremendous financial strain on the fledgling business. The company, which started with so much potential, suddenly found itself drowning in legal and financial troubles, and it wouldn't be long before the men found themselves before a judge in bankruptcy court.

The legal proceedings marked the end of the Buffalo Italian Importing Company. Whether the three men knew about the shady practices or not, the short-lived venture only marked the beginning for Giuseppe DiCarlo. This was a man who had a mind for business and a knack for strategy, but a great mind alone couldn't get the proper foundation set. For that, he would need someone to put their feet on the pavement while he sat back and pulled the strings. Fortune would favor DiCarlo, as he didn't have to wait long for that person.

The Start of the Buffalo Crime Family

Fate would eventually bring the two halves together, changing the course for the city of Buffalo. Angelo Palmeri married Rosaria Mistretta on October 5, 1913. Rosaria, though, was the cousin of Vicenza DiCarlo, the wife of one Giuseppe DiCarlo. That wedding would be a significant spark for what was to come.

As the year came to an end, Angelo and Rosaria would make a decision that would solidify what started with the wedding. They moved into an apartment located above the DiCarlo family home on Seventh Street. The families would be close, but that move formed a camaraderie between Angelo and Giuseppe. Their friendship started with a personal rapport, but it grew into a mutual respect as the two realized they shared many of the same interests. This personal bond would eventually grow into a business partnership, which was centered in the confines of Palmeri's tavern.

In this partnership, Angelo Palmeri would hand the reins over to DiCarlo. However, he was not without power; he served as an underboss to the DiCarlo organization. He was an advisor and an enforcer—it was a crucial role that fit him perfectly. Angelo provided the necessary support to ensure that the organization ran as smoothly as possible. DiCarlo, now sitting as the leader, got to strategize comfortably, knowing that Palmeri would ensure things were done. It was a new chapter in Buffalo, one with shared responsibilities and mutual growth.

The pairing of Palmeri and DiCarlo was largely characterized by the stark contrasts in how they conducted business. However, that contrast is what made their organization effective. DiCarlo was able to mastermind the expansion of the family, ensuring their growth and influence. He took the helm and made the crucial decisions that shaped an empire that lasted generations.

Meanwhile, Angelo was playing the role of enforcer. It was up to him to keep the rest of the family in line, ensuring that everything that was done adhered to the rules and regulations of the organization and the Mafia as a whole. Palmeri was the strong arm that maintained order and discipline.

While it was an ideal partnership, Angelo was still making waves. His violent nature and love for the American Wild West earned him the nickname "Buffalo Bill." He was not the type of person to shy away from using force when necessary, which gave him quite the reputation. That same violent nature would eventually catch up to him. In 1915, Angelo was arrested yet again; this time for assaulting a police officer.

The Years of Success

A few short months after Angelo was arrested, a small ray of sun peeked through the chaos. He and Rosaria welcomed their daughter into the world. Her baptism in November was an occasion filled with joy, and Joseph (Giuseppe's son) and Sarah DiCarlo served as godparents to the little girl. This ceremony only strengthened the bonds between the Palmeri and DiCarlo families.

The joy would quickly fade away for Palmeri though, as Rosaria fell victim to a brutal one-two punch of influenza and pneumonia. On January 5, 1916, at just 29 years old, Rosaria Palmeri died. Angelo was overcome with grief from losing his wife, and during that grief, he realized that he couldn't raise their daughter alone. It was a difficult choice, but he decided to send his daughter to live with Rosaria's parents in New York City.

Still devastated, Angelo couldn't face returning to Buffalo, so he took a break from the city, finding some solace thirty minutes away in Niagara Falls. Here, he opened a cigar store, but beneath the legitimate business lurked a familiar presence—he was part of the mafia after all. The cigar shop would be a front for the family's gambling operations. It seemed like a perfect combination, and it does leave one very interesting point to note too. A young Willie Moretti, who would become a notorious figure in the Genovese family of New York City, was honing his craft by running craps games for Angelo—a testament to the training grounds that the underbosses provided.

1919 would begin a new chapter for Angelo. He found a new flame and comfort in his new wife, Rosaria's older sister, Loretta. His and Rosaria's daughter joined them as he moved the family to an apartment in Niagara Falls. By then, it was the age of Prohibition, a golden ticket for the criminal empires in America, and the DiCarlo-Palmeri family wasn't going to pass up this lucrative racket.

Angelo wouldn't be alone either. Besides his new wife and his daughter, Angelo would join forces with his brother Paul to manage the bootlegging empire. They would join hands with a more-than-formidable crew—the Sirianni brothers, Don Simone Borruso,

Joseph Sottile, and Rocco Perri, the Canadian mob boss. This was a mafia dream team, and the alliance would become a juggernaut, bringing outlawed alcohol across the border from Canada. Niagara Falls, a place of serenity and scenic wonder, had just become one of the largest hubs in this illicit trade.

Angelo navigated this venture as he had every venture before. It was a great start for the family, and they would see plenty of money flow in, but it wasn't quite where it needed to be. The racket would need a stronger leader to really see the revenue explode. They also needed that leader because bootlegging came with a large cost. Mafia families that were smuggling and distributing alcohol had massive targets painted on their backs. Not only did they have an outraged public and law enforcement breathing down their necks, but rivals and upstart gangs also eyed the territory, wanting a piece for themselves.

The Decline

1921 wouldn't be too kind to Angelo Palmeri either. He found himself facing yet another accusation: This time for the murder of one Emilio Gnazzo. The murder itself was a textbook back-alley job. Gnazzo was jumped from behind and shot; however, there was a sole witness to the murder—Emilio Gnazzo's wife. The widow immediately named Palmeri as the triggerman. The cops swarmed in, started the investigation, and would uncover a damning motive for the murder. Gnazzo had taken out a hefty loan and was behind on payments. His creditor was none other than Angelo Palmeri, which meant Palmeri's luck had run out.

But fate and the Mafia worked in mysterious ways. As the case finally made its way to trial, Gnazzo's wife, the key witness for the prosecution's case, vanished. The woman was nowhere to be found, and without a single piece of corroborating evidence or another witness to come forward, the case was a wash. Palmeri had once again slipped through the grasp of the law. While he walked free, there was still a dark cloud over him; perhaps the proof that he wouldn't be fit to take over DiCarlo's spot when the time came.

Meanwhile, back down in Buffalo, the time for Giuseppe DiCarlo was coming fast as his world began to unravel. Tuberculosis was running rampant at the time and had taken hold of the boss, siphoning his energy and leaving behind a shell of the once vibrant leader. As if that wasn't enough of a shot to the DiCarlo family, death would come calling for his brother, claimed by the same disease that would kill Giuseppe. Then, to deal the biggest blow to him, his wife Vicenza lost her battle with cancer. The cool, calculated leader of the Buffalo Crime Family had no will to keep going.

With everything happening with Giuseppe, coupled with the run of bad luck that constantly found Palmeri, one thing had become abundantly clear: A power shift was imminent in Buffalo, and there was one up-and-comer that outshined everyone, Stefano Magaddino.

In July 1922, Giuseppe DiCarlo's reign had come to an end. The boss's death drew Angelo and his family back to the city of Buffalo, where he assumed temporary control of the family. Even Angelo knew that he wouldn't make for a good leader and that his control was a stop-gap measure until the family could decide on the next leader. The ruthless understudy Magaddino would soon get the vote of confidence. Palmeri, along with the likes of Filippo Mazzara and Giuseppe DiBenedetto—who were all Castellammarese Mafiosi held leadership roles under DiCarlo—simply transitioned their roles to the new regime. The changing of the guard had been completed, and the most successful chapter of the Buffalo Mafia's story would unfold.

The Palmeri-DiCarlo Legacy

Palmeri would continue for the next decade, even becoming a naturalized citizen of the United States in January 1925. Five years later Palmeri would support Salvatore Maranzano when the Castellammarese War broke out in 1930. However, toward the end of the bloody power struggle, Angelo faced increasingly severe health problems and died of a stroke in December 1932.

Although their years in power were brief, it was this partnership that was the turning point for the Buffalo Mafia. This period, while a far cry from the more sophisticated operations that the Mafia would later develop, was one of explosive growth. It was like the Wild West that Palmeri loved, full of brutal competition and rivalries settled by bullets and bloodshed.

But it wasn't all violence and money. No successful organization would survive without honor, and that was something that Angelo Palmeri and Giuseppe DiCarlo would display. Despite their contrasting styles, they shared a similar vision and remained loyal to each other. This would be a huge cornerstone in the family's code for decades to come, and their honor would also have a softer side. The often-violent Palmeri would use his influence within the

Sicilian community to provide aid to the devastated family of a boy who had been slain by a drifter in 1925. Angelo, along with other underbosses, took donations from shopkeepers to fund the funeral expenses and offer other assistance to the family.

The legacy of Palmeri and DiCarlo lived on in the efficient and effective leadership of Stefano Magaddino and even in the leaders of today. But now the focus turns to that one up-and-comer who rose through the ranks and turned the Buffalo crime family into the Magaddino Crime Family.

PART II
THE MAGADDINO ERA
(1922-1980S)

CHAPTER 2

THE EARLY YEARS OF STEFANO MAGADDINO

Stefano "The Undertaker" Magaddino was born under a blanket of violence on October 10, 1891, in Castellammare del Golfo, Sicily. The streets of his hometown were buzzing with the sounds of a feud that had been spanning generations. Stefano was the third of Giovanni and Giuseppa Magaddino's eight children, and he was born at a time when the Magaddino family and their relatives were in an ongoing, bitter feud with the Buccellato clan. Violence wasn't a distant threat for a young Stefano; instead, it was a harsh reality that would influence his childhood.

While he would end up on the other side of this later, initially, he was privy to hushed conversations that were rooted in fear. That fear hung thick in the Sicilian air, but amidst the ever-present terror, the seeds of loyalty would flourish. Stefano witnessed the price some paid for their unwavering, misplaced alliance, which was often collected in blood. He also learned about the chilling chess game of revenge, a lesson he would become very familiar with. This "baptism by violence" was brutal, but it would forever shape the person Magaddino would become.

His formative years would be steeped in the shadowy structure of the Sicilian underworld, where Stefano would experiment with some low-level crimes. Every lesson and every brutal encounter during this time would be a brick laid in the Magaddino foundation. In 1909, right as he was on the edge of manhood and falling into deeper trouble, an 18-year-old Stefano left Castellammare for the quickly growing Mafia landscape in New York City.

He found himself surrounded by familiarity, though, in Brooklyn's Williamsburg. This wasn't a chance landing either; it was a Castellammarese hotspot, an area controlled by the Bonannos, another Castellammare clan, to whom the Magaddinos were bound by blood. There would be no time for late-teenage awkwardness, as Stefano found himself knee-deep in the New York Mafia scene.

He was already sharp and displayed immense loyalty, which caught the eye of Giuseppe "Joe Bananas" Bonanno. Stefano quickly carved out his own place as an advisor and a street enforcer. The combination of fists and cunning would help the Bonannos solidify their empire in the city. This was still in the "Wild West" years of the mafia, which were some of the most violent years, and Stefano was in the middle of it all, proving to be a rising star.

While it was a rush of chaos, Stefano would find a bit of normalcy in 1913 when he married Carmela Caroddo. His brother Gaspare followed suit soon after, marrying Carmela's sister. It was a slight reminder that loyalty went well beyond blood ties for the Mafia.

That normalcy would likely help Stefano keep a level head because at this time the Mafia presence in New York City was a fractured mess. There were various competing factions all trying to assert their dominance. It was because of this that Stefano would find another group, one that was feared and ruthless. They were known simply as the "Good Killers," and they weren't the average Mafia muscle. These were almost like the hitmen's hitmen, the ones that families called on for delicate matters and permanent solutions. Stefano, equipped with his growing reputation for efficiency and cold resolve, caught their eye. This crew was the embodiment of everything the Mafia was, and it was where Stefano thrived.

It was within this group that Stefano Magaddino developed his skills until they were razor-sharp. He learned the criminal art of the silent takedown, which is when a victim would disappear before the bullet left the chamber. Of all the defining moments in his younger years, this was the period that made the man who would go on to become "The Undertaker," the figure that was seen as the king of the Buffalo underworld. He wouldn't know it yet, but something was brewing in his former home, which would be the catalyst that put him on the path to Buffalo.

The Good Killers' Case

The following is a rare piece of evidence that the Good Killers existed in the history of the Mafia, and it paints a truly chilling picture of the underworld, where anything but fierce loyalty comes with the most severe consequences. In the end, Stefano Magaddino was still well on his way to being the head of the Buffalo Crime Family. However, this brush with the law could have severely altered the course of Mafia history.

The Murder of Pietro Magaddino

Around 1916, the atmosphere in Sicily was packed with tension. It was as if a dense fog of uncertainty and mistrust had fallen over a landscape that was already ready to become a violent storm. This storm would be one of a brutal battle, which would change the life of the future leader of the Buffalo Crime Family forever. It was in this violent skirmish that the life of Stefano's brother, Pietro Magaddino, would be claimed. Shockwaves were sent through Stefano's expanding world.

Stefano was naturally consumed by immense grief in the beginning. While it came with the territory of the mafioso lifestyle, he still devastatingly lost his brother. So, more than the loss, it was the nature of Pietro's death that was even more unbearable. However, as time moved forward, Stefano's mourning turned into something else—rage and an extremely loud cry for retribution. It wasn't an uncommon reaction in the criminal underworld or for anyone who lost a family member like that. It was almost expected, but Stefano didn't know who deserved his wrath. There were rumors, discussions, and a vast number of accusations thrown around about who could have killed Pietro.

It wouldn't take long for a solid lead to emerge from the chaos, and that came in the form of Camillo Caiozzo. Camillo was a low-level thug in the Sicilian Mafia, but he would become infamous when he was named as an accomplice in Pietro's murder. News of Stefano's retribution had already reached Camillo, which immediately put him in a state of fear. He knew what awaited him in Sicily for even being involved in Pietro Magaddino's murder. Vengeance was essentially a Sicilian birthright, and it was a shadow that would hang over his head until someone made the move to strike.

The fear was too much for Caiozzo to bear, so he decided to take his chances on fleeing. He needed refuge, and the only place where he could think of laying low was in the hustle and bustle of New York City. Perhaps Caiozzo thought that Buffalo and New York City were far enough apart, or maybe he thought that he could maintain a level of anonymity among the throngs of people. No matter what his thinking, the wheels were already in motion and Camillo Caiozzo's life was on contract. It was just a matter of time.

Stefano's Vengeance

In the aftermath of Pietro's death, Stefano Magaddino was hellbent on vengeance. He was a man possessed, consumed by a singular desire to avenge his brother's murder. Word had gotten back to him that Camillo Caiozzo was in America, likely walking the streets of New York City, waiting for things to die down. Stefano could have struck quickly, but he was patient. He would hold back, biding his time until the moment was just right.

The year was 1921, and New York City was a bustling place where a person really could disappear into a crowd. It was also a city where a secret could be made, except this wouldn't be a secret for long. In the most mafioso, unassuming way, Caiozzo met his bloody end. The execution was silent and effective. Stefano Magaddino had gotten his revenge, and he had just sent a clear message to anyone who dared cross him or the Good Killers. As long as no one spoke of what happened, it would be a done deal.

Time passed, allowing the memory of Caiozzo's disappearance (likely murder) to fade into the background. However, fate would have a way of bringing misdeeds to light. In the secluded cove of Shark River in New Jersey, a gruesome discovery was made. Lying with the driftwood that washed ashore was the lifeless body of Camillo Caiozzo. The chilling discovery served as a stern reminder that the Mafia's code of conduct wasn't a myth but a brutal reality. It was an eye for an eye.

The discovery of the body wasn't surprising. It's what came after that sent shockwaves through the underworld. This was a twist that no one saw coming.

A New Jersey barber named Bartolo Fontana walked into a police station, ready to tell them everything that he knew and had done. He confessed to being the triggerman who carried out the hit on Caiozzo, only two weeks before the body was found in the cove. The police were already accustomed to the inner workings of the Mafia, but they weren't ready for what Fontana would do next.

Fontana didn't stop at just confessing his role in the murder. He took it a step further by selling out the Good Killers. He admitted that while he did act alone in the murder, he had done so following the orders passed to him by the Magaddino-led criminal outfit. He pinned Stefano as the person who had been the mastermind behind the killing. This revelation would send a shockwave through the criminal underworld, and things were about to turn upside down.

The Sting and the Trial

Bartolo Fontana was highly aware of the dangerous path he had chosen to take. He, like many, knew all too well that anyone who dared to sell out a mafioso wouldn't live to tell the tale. The knowledge that his being cooperative with law enforcement would paint a massive target on his back that would eat at the barber. It was a jail sentence or a death sentence—Bartolo was between a rock and a hard place. But the looming threat of retaliation (and sure death) from the Good Killers that hung over Bartolo led him to choose to take a deal with the police. The deal would come in the form of a sting operation in which Fontana would act as the bait that would lure Stefano and the rest of the crew into a well-placed trap. The police saw it as a golden opportunity to unveil the Good Killers, and it could have rewritten the entire story of Stefano Magaddino and the Buffalo Crime Family.

The stage had been set for the sting operation. It would happen at the famed Grand Central Station, where Fontana would play the role of a terrified hitman looking to skip town and lay low. It was a legitimate front, as a killer would be terrified that their target's body had been found floating in the New Jersey water. He arranged the meeting with Stefano, looking for any help in fleeing. It was a tense exchange, with Fontana hoping that he wouldn't raise any of Magaddino's suspicion. The only thing Stefano saw, though, was someone desperate for help. He was so convinced of the barber's fear that he offered him $30 to leave town. As the bills exchanged hands, undercover cops swooped in and nabbed Stefano. Subsequently, four other members of the good killers were arrested, effectively bringing the group's activity to a screeching halt.

The threat of retaliation was a distant memory for Fontana, which emboldened him to reveal even more about the Good Killers. He gave the court as many details of the outfit and their activities as he could recall, including a hit previously executed on Detroit mafioso Felive Buccellato that took place in 1917. Again, he pinned Stefano Magaddino as the man who orchestrated the hit. Law enforcement, prosecutors, and even Bartolo Fontana himself all believed that they had done everything they needed to do to put Stefano and his crew away for good. However, justice had many different plans.

For reasons unknown—and those that favored the future crime boss—the state of New Jersey decided against pressing charges in the murder of Camillo Caiozzo. It was a resounding decision that left even the New York Police, who had meticulously organized the sting operation, stunned. Stefano and the other members of the Good Killers walked scot-free. Meanwhile, Bartolo Fontana was the only one to suffer any real consequences from the ordeal, as he was sentenced to 20 years in prison for Camillo's murder.

Becoming the Undertaker

The legacy of the Good Killers as a Sicilian secret society would fade from the minds of the public because there was much more activity from the criminal underworld to focus on. Magaddino narrowly slipped through the fingers of the law, and now with the taste of freedom, he left the New York courtroom a changed man. While he was already a strong leader, he was still naive. Stefano was still a young immigrant looking to cement his place in the United States. But now, he was more of a cunning operator who wanted more than just an underboss role, like he had a score to settle.

He spent some of his time after the trial traveling across the US, but it wouldn't be long before he found himself back in New York. Except, he found his place in the northwest corner, close to the Canadian border. Stefano found Buffalo—a city that was booming while still rough around the edges, much like Magaddino.

Magaddino would set up shop in nearby Niagara Falls, which would ultimately be the Buffalo family's most lucrative move. Nestled among the industrial smokestacks and the harbors, Stefano opened the Magaddino Memorial Chapel. It was a symbol of death, but it was also a symbol of Magaddino's fresh start. This building would earn him the nickname "The Undertaker," which seemed to serve as a reminder of the line that he toed throughout his life. The funeral home wasn't a facade though. Like several operations, it was a legitimate front, but death wouldn't be the only business booming in the 1920s. Prohibition was now on the tip of everyone's tongue, and although there were many supporters, there were just as many people willing to break the law to quench this newfound thirst. Magaddino, ever the strategist, saw a tremendous opportunity.

Magaddino's funeral home was positioned so close to the Canadian border that it made for the perfect place for a much more prosperous endeavor. With Prohibition stopping at the US border, Magaddino saw his chance to enter the bootlegging racket. The booze that was high in demand made a slow but steady flow into the United States. Canadian affiliates would load crates of alcohol onto rickety boats and sail under the cover of darkness. Once the boats were safely on American soil, the crates were swiftly moved to warehouses, back alleys, or funeral homes. The alcohol would then make it to the speakeasies in the area. Jazz clubs and piano bars served as a front for Magaddino's biggest steps in the criminal underworld. With every clinking glass, Stefano Magaddino became that much more of an influence on the region.

It was more than just about lining his pockets and finding a piece of the "good life," although that was a great perk. The bootlegging racket was just a foot in the door, a way to get deeper into the underbelly of organized crime. He found that way in by working up through the ranks of the DiCarlo family. Magaddino took his already exceptional skills and honed them. While he was a great underboss who knew the delicate dance of loyalty and betrayal, he would prove to the rest of the DiCarlo-Palmeri family that he was ready for more. That ruthlessness and cunning nature kept him well ahead of his enemies and saw him quickly seated at the top of potential successors of the Buffalo family when the time was right.

Magaddino wouldn't have to wait long. DiCarlo's health was already in rapid decline, and his death would create that opening for Magaddino. There was no question that the role of boss would fall on Magaddino's shoulders. It was time for the DiCarlo-Palmeri Family to shed its old skin and emerge as the Magaddino Crime Family, a name that would become synonymous with power and influence in the city of Buffalo.

Once a sleepy town in the northwest corner of New York, Buffalo would soon become a hub of the American Mafia. Now, under the iron fist of Magaddino, the family was ready to grow and diversify. Bootlegging would remain a cornerstone, like with many families, but Stefano knew that they would need to dip into other rackets to remain on top. With a new leader, the family wouldn't just be out to make money. They were out of control, ready to tighten their grip and interweave themselves into every aspect of life in Buffalo.

CHAPTER 3
THE REIGN OF THE MAGADDINO CRIME FAMILY

In the expansive history of the American criminal underworld, few names have the same type of power as that of Stefano Magaddino—despite his name not being mentioned alongside your typical Mafia bosses. That said, Magaddino wasn't your typical Mafia boss. He was a man who had already taken on leadership roles, exhibiting an icy ruthlessness that set him apart from other figures in the mafia. While other bosses were characterized by flamboyance and living in the glitz and glamor of it all, Stefano was molded by a lifetime of experience, making him a quiet cunning force.

Taking control of the Buffalo family was an easy decision for the underbosses to make, and it was one that would have effects that were felt even outside the region. This wasn't a simple change in leadership, it was a shift that would propel the organization to unforeseen heights. The Buffalo Crime Family had a solid beginning under the control of Giuseppe DiCarlo, but they were about to enter the Magaddino era.

The next decade for the Buffalo—now the Magaddino—Crime Family would be a blur of cunning, strategic maneuvers. This period would be marked by bloody alliances and shattered loyalty, and it was all done in the pursuit of prosperity. That pursuit would leave behind a lot of enemies and those who couldn't adapt in its wake. There were triumphs and setbacks, but this would be the era that defined the Buffalo underworld.

Expansion and Power Plays

Again, Magaddino was a man of quiet authority, so he wasn't one to flaunt his power around. However, his actions spoke volumes about his leadership and his vision for the future. In 1923, after securing the mantle of leadership, he made a significant move that helped define the direction in which the organization would go. This was done by bringing in his brother Antonio over from their Sicilian breeding grounds of Castellammare. Antonio quickly became a valuable asset to the organization, and he would take his place as a trusted confidante and advisor to Stefano.

Together, the Magaddino brothers set up their headquarters in Niagara Falls. This maneuver was far more than just about Stefano staying close to home; it was a clear declaration of intent. The Magaddino family was staking its claim on the prime location for the booming bootlegging racket. As control was solidified in Niagara Falls, their underbosses (Angelo Palmeri, Filippo Mazzara, and the others from the DiCarlo days) fortified the hold in Buffalo. It was a coordinated effort that ensured that the family's grip wasn't on just a city but on the entire northwest region of New York.

While power struggles were a common thing in New York City, the Magaddino Crime Family took control over the area. Their strategic positioning and meticulous planning helped them curb a lot of the chaos and focus on the expansion of their operations.

An extremely calculative move followed soon after when Stefano became a naturalized citizen of the US in 1923. The act, while a natural event for many immigrants, would work well in favor of Stefano's reign. For many of the lower-ranking members of the Mafia, brushes with authorities would result in deportation. Deportation caused delays in operations, and that spelled trouble if you were in any type of leadership role. However, Stefano's citizenship gave him a secure base, allowing him to operate without that particular fear.

This newfound security allowed Stefano to expand into more legitimate businesses, all of which served as a smokescreen for his criminal empire. He worked under the radar while expanding his empire. It seemed everything Stefano was doing was a testament to his genius, especially as the family's image and revenue were significantly boosted.

The Magaddino family's rise to power wasn't chance or luck. There were no meetings of fate. This was the result of careful planning, strategic moves, and Stefano's shrewd decision-making. The boss's leadership, coupled with the support of strong underbosses, allowed the organization to establish a tight grip. What followed was an explosion of underworld success.

Bootlegging Gold

The 18th Amendment

Any look at the golden age of the American Mafia would point you right toward the Prohibition era and the days of bootlegging. The 18th Amendment, which banned the manufacture, sale, and transportation of alcohol inadvertently created the perfect environment for the criminal underworld, including the American Mafia to thrive. While there were plenty of people who were pro-18th Amendment, there were also those who had a demand for alcohol.

The Mafia, with its well-structured hierarchy and incredible efficiency, established sophisticated bootlegging operations. They brought in alcohol from places like Canada and the Caribbean, and they would then distribute it through networks of speakeasies and illegal bars, often touted as jazz clubs and other legitimate establishments. It was a time of great wealth, influence, and power for any crime family. It was also a time for power struggles and gang wars.

Moreover, the Prohibition era exposed widespread corruption in law enforcement and politicians during this time. Many would be "in the pockets" of the crime families, turning a blind eye in exchange for bribes (be it cash or other favors). This allowed the organizations to operate with impunity, and many would use these figures to rid themselves of any potential threats to their profits.

It was a chaotic period in American history, and the city of Buffalo was no exception either.

Magaddino's Role in the Alcohol Racket

In these early days of the Prohibition Era, luck (probably in the form of some well-greased wheels) smiled on the Magaddino Crime Family. While the United States was dried out, the sale and consumption of alcohol was still very much legal across the Canadian border. The geographical advantage made Buffalo a haven for anyone wanting to get into the lucrative bootlegging game. DiCarlo and Palmeri recognized that and had already exploited the positioning, but now with a new leader, things were about to grow exponentially.

Not one to overlook a golden opportunity, Magaddino exploited their advantage as much as he could. The family became the gatekeepers of the liquor coming in from Canada, deciding which cities received the precious booze and which were cut off. Control like this not only made the local speakeasies conform to the rules set by the Magaddino family, but it also ensured the surrounding areas followed suit. The Magaddino organization's influence spread rapidly, and their power was felt well outside their territory.

Stefano's cold, calculated nature played a huge role in this expansion. He ruled with an iron fist, ensuring that the family ran efficiently. If DiCarlo was a great strategist, it would make Magaddino a master of the craft given his ability to make tough decisions when necessary. Under Stefano's leadership, the Buffalo region had money and power that would rival any of the notorious gangsters.

That power would also be a deterrent for anyone who dared to cross into Magaddino territory. The family had a reputation for ruthlessness and the way they would show their control over the liquor racket made them a formidable force. Magaddino and his underbosses, especially Palmeri, would swiftly deal with anyone who tried to challenge them or attempt to operate in their territory.

The Magaddino Family's rise to prominence during the chaotic prohibition years was a testament to superb leadership, strategic planning, and no hesitation to execute those plans (along with a few foes too). They could spot the opportunities presented to them, just like the geographical positioning of Buffalo, and use them to their fullest advantage. Buffalo would become one of the strongholds in the liquor trade, which was one of the most lucrative trades for the Mafia. Not everyone would appreciate the Magaddino family's newfound prosperity though.

The result of that displeasure, combined with growing tensions within the families of New York City, would lead the way for the Castellammarese War. Named after the Sicilian town where Magaddino and many other members of the American Mafia were born, this war was a bloody power struggle for control of the American Mafia. Lasting for just over a year, it would be the very catalyst needed for a major change in the landscape of the criminal underworld.

Castellammarese War and the Commission

By the late 1920s, the American Mafia was controlled by Giuseppe "Joe the Boss" Masseria. His faction consisted of gangsters from Sicily, Calabria, and Campania, and while there were power struggles within the Mafia, things ran largely uninterrupted. That was until bootlegging was winding down, meaning that competition was becoming more intense over the smuggling racket.

Masseria looked at the Magaddino family and other Castellammarese mafiosos as a growing threat. To him, their operations were acts of rebellion; therefore, he summoned family leaders, including Magaddino, to New York City. This was a not-so-subtle power move, and Stefano knew it as such. The intimidating Buffalo leader never took kindly to being intimidated by anyone else, and he wasn't about to start now. He refused to make the trip to New York City for the meeting, which only enraged Masseria. This refusal led Masseria to call for the murder of Magaddino.

The Landscape of the War

Don Vito Ferro, a powerful Sicilian Don, looked to take control of the American Mafia operations, so he sent Castellammare native Salvatore Maranzano to do so. Stefano Magaddino was a key figure in the Castellammarese faction, which meant he had an alliance with Maranzano. This would also mean that his alliances and refusal to meet with Masseria would be a significant contributor to the war.

However, jumping back just slightly, the Castellammarese War wasn't just a Mafia power struggle between Joe the Boss and Maranzano. The war itself was the culmination of a generational conflict between the older Sicilian leadership, known as the "Mustache Petes" and the "Young Turks," a younger, diverse group of Italian-Americans. The Mustache Petes were traditionalists; they wanted to hold on to the things they brought from Sicily and refused to conduct business with non-Italians. But the Young Turks, under the leadership of one Charles "Lucky" Luciano, wanted to modernize the mob. They also wanted to put an end to the constant in-fighting and resume their businesses.

Tensions finally boiled over when Masseria called for the murder of Gaspar Milazzo, a Castellammarese native who had not shown his support during one of many disputes. This common act, though, marked the beginning of the war. Things escalated more when Masseria also ordered a hit on ally Gaetano Reina, which would protect Masseria's secret allies. However, this betrayal of the Reina family saw their support move from Masseria to Maranzano.

The war became increasingly violent with blood spilling out on the streets of New York City. It seemed that things would wind down, though, when Joe the Boss was assassinated in April 1931. Salvatore Maranzano saw the opening and took over Masseria's position. Maranzano would create the Five Families of New York, giving each family a territory and a structured hierarchy. It was an overall beneficial move for the Mafia, but there were already issues with the new capo.

Maranzano's leadership was overshadowed by his arrogance, greed, and paranoia. What really drove the other families over the edge, though, was when he demanded that the Five Families pay him tribute. A rebellion was ignited and under orders from Lucky Luciano, a hit was put out on Maranzano. Five months after his reign as capo began, Maranzano was assassinated similarly to his predecessor.

It was clear as the Castellammarese War progressed that the old ways of the Mafia were no longer sustainable. That became even more obvious when Maranzano took control. The Young Turks saw a need for change and were going to take drastic steps to achieve it.

Lucky Luciano's vision of the mob was an attractive one to many followers, especially those who saw many glaring faults with Masseria's leadership. The War would see fluid factions and several members switching sides or killing allies.

The war had finally ended with the assassination of Maranzano, which meant that change could come to fruition. That change transformed the American Mafia from the rough and tumble era to the syndicate that we know today.

Aftermath and the Commission

In the aftermath of the bloody war, Lucky Luciano, the visionary of the American Mafia, also realized that there were inherent dangers in having one unchallenged leader. It needed to be addressed, so Luciano called for a meeting in Chicago with the most influential figures of the Mafia, including Stefano Magaddino. The attendees made the journey with the expectation that Luciano would claim the role of Capo. While there would have been little to no disagreement about the move, those in attendance were shocked when Luciano eliminated the position. Instead, he proposed a radically different structure that would be known as the Commission.

The Commission would be much akin to a Mafia board of directors, a governing body that would oversee all Mafia activity across the country. There would be seven seats on this board, five seats held by the leaders of the Five Families, Chicago's Al Capone, and Buffalo's Stefano Magaddino. Putting this structure in place would democratize power within the entire Mafia, and the members of the Commission would become mediators in any disputes. They would also get to have the final say in leadership appointments.

Luciano drafted this proposal to be a power-sharing agreement, which would prevent future bloodshed and effectively resolve any internal conflict. While the role was abolished, Luciano was positioned as a silent capo. He would be more of a guiding hand instead of an arrogant leader. The bosses all agreed to the innovative approach, and so the Commission was born. The group agreed to meet every five years or whenever there were any important matters that needed to be addressed. And this was the turning point in the history of the American Mafia. The Commission brought organization and governance, something that was previously absent and something that would be needed for the future of the criminal underworld.

Triumphs and Setbacks

Despite the new structure for the American mafia with the Commission, tension within the New York families would continue. However, Magaddino wasn't going to back down from any challenge. He called on fear as his weapon. He had enforcers who were known for their brutality, which put a sense of terror into any potential rivals. If there were whispers of dissent, they would be met swiftly and with severe consequences. Stefano Magaddino wasn't just a one-trick pony though. He understood the power of "greasing the wheels." A little bribe here and a strategic relationship with a politician there were some common tactics that Magaddino used to ensure cooperation or a blind eye from people in positions of authority. He also knew how to infiltrate labor unions, which gave him even more of a hold on the region with power over key industries and their workforces.

Meanwhile, prohibition was becoming a double-edged sword, bringing great triumphs and crippling setbacks. While bootlegging was flourishing with the roaring '20s generating unheard-of profits for the Magaddino family, crackdowns from law enforcement began to ramp up. There was also a tremendous public backlash against the illegal liquor trade. Of course, the racket would take a much bigger blow when the 1929 stock market crash crippled the economy.

Magaddino, though, was a proactive strategist and had prepared for such challenges. The family had already started to diversify their portfolio by joining the gambling racket and other underworld activities. This may have been the foresight that would ensure the family would carry on, even as the sun began to set on the Prohibition Era and bootlegging.

By the end of the 1920s and the early 1930s, Stefano Magaddino took DiCarlo and Palmeri's foundation and built a powerful force in the criminal underworld. He navigated an explosive decade that was rife with family wars, political leveraging, and economic instability. With his effective combination of ruthlessness, cunning, and forged alliances, he didn't just set the family up for decades of success but also set himself up to be the head of the family during that success.

The abolishment of Prohibition in 1933 would bring in a new era, one that would bring its own set of challenges and new opportunities. However, for the Buffalo leader, whom they called the Undertaker, the 1930s were still just the beginning of the crime family's growth and stranglehold over Buffalo.

CHAPTER 4

THE MAGADDINO FAMILY AFTER PROHIBITION

The End of Prohibition

As the Prohibition Era wound down and finally came to a close with the repeal of the 18th Amendment in 1933, the Magaddino Crime family firmly established their dominance in the northwestern region of New York. The family successfully navigated the rough waters of this explosive time of bootlegging and violent infighting and capitalized on the opportunities that were presented, thereby expanding their criminal empire.

Stefano, the shrewd and efficient leader, managed to guide the Buffalo family through the yearlong Castellammarese War, and his effectiveness as a leader landed him a seat on the Commission. Being a part of the new governing body that oversaw the American Mafia was an incredible feat, allowing him to further influence Mafia activities across the US and not just in Buffalo.

During the days of Prohibition, the Magaddino family was well-positioned again and became heavily involved in bootlegging operations. However, as the era came to an end, the family quickly adapted and diversified their criminal activities. They would expand into other areas of crime, including gambling and racketeering, which allowed them to maintain their vice-like grip on the region, even as the lucrative days of alcohol smuggling faded into the night.

Gambling operations became a significant source of revenue for the family. The Magaddino organization operated numerous gambling dens and ran multiple bookmaking operations, some of which were even operating within horse racing tracks. It goes without question that the family had reach and influence. Their hold on the gambling world in northwest New York not only gave them income but also allowed them to influence the way the chips fell.

Racketeering was another major source of income for the family. This aspect of business involved collecting money from businesses and individuals in return for Magaddino's protection. Oftentimes, the dues were simply granting these businesses the ability to operate in what would otherwise be mafia territory. If sufficient dues were not paid, threats of violence would fall on those businesses or people. With Magaddino's rule, there would be no second warnings, ensuring that anyone living in the family's territory would pay up.

As the end of Prohibition loomed, there were also hints of the family venturing into drug trafficking. While it wasn't a major operation at this stage for much of the Mafia, it was clear that eyes fell on any potential source of revenue. With changes in politics later down the line, and the changes in American culture, drug trafficking became a significant part of criminal operations.

The end of Prohibition marked a major turning point for the Magaddino Crime Family. They had successfully navigated through some of the biggest challenges that were presented to the Mafia while also successfully expanding their operations. Stefano solidified their position, making them a dominant part of the Mafia as they pushed on to a new period of American history. It was his leadership and strategic foresight that allowed these changes to happen.

The Impact of the Magaddino Family

The operations of the Magaddino family had a huge impact on Buffalo, Niagara Falls, and the surrounding communities. While almost all of their activities were illicit, they still contributed to the local economy in several ways. The gambling dens and speakeasies they operated (even as Prohibition was repealed) employed several residents. Many of these establishments also served as places of entertainment, providing a brief moment of normalcy from the harsh realities of life during the Great Depression.

In addition to their typical Mafia operations, the Magaddino family also engaged in philanthropic endeavors. It's typically overlooked how much Mafia organizations positively contributed to their communities. While it doesn't negate the criminal aspect of their operations, they would donate to local charities and fund community projects—all aimed at improving public infrastructure and services. This philanthropy, along with other economic contributions would sway some public perception in their favor. This is particularly true when many families were struggling to just get by.

However, while some of these charitable actions were wholesome, these activities were often part of a bigger strategy put forth by the Mafia families. They used their wealth to boost the local economy, which would gain them social capital and more influence throughout the communities they controlled. While specifics of the Magaddino contributions aren't clear, many families would sponsor local sports teams or provide scholarships for local students. Of course, many would donate to political campaigns, either gaining the influence of politicians in place or putting politicians that they favored into positions of power.

Again, while everything was seemingly harmless, their community outreach gave them leverage to maintain control over their territories and safeguard their criminal enterprise. By integrating themselves with the community, local authorities, and politicians, they could operate with little to no interference.

Yet not everyone celebrated the organization or even was on board with the long and ominous shadow that the Magaddino family cast over the northwestern region of New York. With their ruthless tactics and a blatant disregard for authority, they became a feared and often loathed presence in the community. Those who opposed the family or refused to fall in line with their demands would usually find themselves at the receiving end of Magaddino's wrath. These feelings were not unfounded, though, nor were they just a reaction to the proximity to the mafia. The Magaddino family was known for the brutal enforcement of their rules, and they were always willing to resort to violence to maintain their grip on the region.

However, the once-blind eye of the authorities toward the family's activities started to fade. With public outcry against the American Mafia beginning to swell across the country, law enforcement agencies, from local agencies to the FBI, were forced to take action against the families. This action also came from these agencies because further inaction would expose that they were complicit or, worse, had alliances with the crime families. So, for much of Stefano's reign, he and the rest of the Magaddino family found themselves as targets of multiple arrests, government investigations, and prosecutions.

The Apalachin Meeting

One such occurrence that showed that law enforcement was cracking down on organized crime came in the form of the Apalachin Meeting. On November 14, 1957, a historic summit of the American Mafia was held. It took place at the home of Joseph "Joe the Barber" Barbara in Apalachin, New York. This meeting would be a significant event in the timeline of organized crime, as it exposed the true existence of the criminal network that sprawled throughout the United States.

The purpose of the meeting was to discuss various topics, including loansharking, gambling, and even the trafficking of narcotics in the country. It was also held to discuss the division of operations that had been under the control of Albert Anastasia, who had been recently murdered. There would be an estimated 100 attendees from the United States, Italy, and even Cuba.

The meeting was originally set to take place in Chicago, but hoping that a change of scenery would ease tensions between families, Magaddino suggested that it be held in Barbara's home. Stefano also suggested the location because he believed the quiet country setting would help them avoid unwanted attention from the law.

However, it was hard for local and state officials to not be suspicious when numerous luxury cars, adorned with license plates from all across the US, began showing up in the normally tranquil Apalachin. Police sat in unmarked cars along the side of the road taking down those license plate numbers. Eventually, a roadblock was set up, and the police would strike, raiding the meeting. Many of the participants fled into the woods and other areas around the Barbara estate. More than 60 bosses were arrested and indicted following the raid.

Around 20 of those bosses who attended the meeting were charged with conspiring to obstruct justice. This came from lying about the nature of this meeting. All of the charged parties were found guilty in January 1959. They were all fined up to $10,000 and given a prison sentence of three to five years. It seemed like the criminal underworld had been dealt a major blow, except all convictions were overturned the following year on appeals.

Again, the most significant outcome of the events was that it confirmed the existence of a nationwide criminal organization. This was a fact that some, including J. Edgar Hoover (director of the Federal Bureau of Investigation), had refused to acknowledge until this point. The Apalachin Meeting also exposed the Mafia to the public that lived outside Mafia-controlled areas, which ramped up the pressure from law enforcement.

Despite the fallout from the Apalachin Meeting, which included the arrest of some of his own members, Stefano managed to maintain his position and avoid any severe consequences for his activity.

This fateful meeting was a game-changing event in the history of organized crime. The mafia and their activities were all exposed and now came under more scrutiny from the general public and law enforcement. However, some, like Magaddino, were still operating "business as usual," which made many wonder if anything could stop the criminal underworld.

The Sign of Descent

Despite the challenges that he faced, Stefano managed to keep a secure grip over the region. He also had the same type of control within the family, which led him to avoid any severe consequences for his criminal activities. It seemed like "The Undertaker" was always just out of reach of the law. However, by no means was this an easy feat. The Magaddino family was far from immune to the changing landscape of the criminal underworld. Like their contemporaries, the Magaddino family had to quickly adapt to increased pressure from law enforcement and the changing public attitude toward organized crime. This meant that every move the family made now would have to be made with the utmost care or everything could collapse on top of them.

Those lessons were proven well before the end of Prohibition when Al Capone was convicted of tax evasion in 1931 after the formation of the Commission. While Capone's position in the public eye didn't help matters, it showed just how quickly an organization could lose everything. This was also seen during the arrests made and the exposure of the Mafia during the Apalachin Meeting. While those flashier figures had exposed their activities, the Mafia as a whole was public knowledge after 1957.

In response to the challenges and threats to their livelihoods, the Magaddino family and other organizations within the American Mafia would look at other avenues to operate. This would lead to many expanding from just racketeering and gambling to loan sharking, extortion, and labor union control. They would also invest money into legitimate businesses in a more subtle way to launder their illegal earnings while maintaining and growing their influence.

From 1933 until around the 1960s, Stefano Magaddino, the effective leader of the Buffalo Crime Family, kept a firm grip on the organization that he had taken over after the death of Guiseppe DiCarlo in 1922. His leadership had spanned decades, and it was a testament to his strategic acumen, ruthless execution of plans, and his constant pursuit of power. It's also attributed to his ability to adapt to any changes that came his way. Magaddino's period of control is one of the longest regimes in the history of the criminal underworld, further cementing the absolute efficiency of his leadership.

However, like all reigns in the criminal underworld, there was an inevitable end. The landscape of the underworld was rapidly changing, especially after the exposure it received due to the massive raid. The 1960s, therefore, posed more challenges to the family's operations in the form of societal shifts, evolving tactics, and increased monitoring from law enforcement. There were even shifts in the internal dynamics of the Mafia and the Magaddino family that started to unravel the strings of control. However, even as these threats to power increased, the family's influence remained significant. This was a true testament to the foundation that was established by DiCarlo and Palmeri.

Stefano Magaddino's leadership style shouldn't be overlooked in the longevity of this reign. The lack of flamboyance, along with his strategic vision, foresight, and adaptability to change elevated him as a leader. He also surrounded himself with a crew of effective underbosses who were key factors in executing his plans and ensuring the family's operations ran smoothly.

While the knowledge of the Magaddino family is limited, this can be seen as just another attribute of their legacy. The reign of the Buffalo Crime Family under Stefano Magaddino is remarkable. Their influence stretched far beyond their bases in Buffalo and Niagara Falls, which helped shape the landscape of organized crime in New York City and beyond. That legacy was well known before the fall of it, but legacy didn't matter in the face of needed change. The world of organized crime in the United States was changing, just as it did in the early 1930s when the Commission took over. How much longer would the powerful Magaddino last as head of the family?

CHAPTER 5

INTERNAL STRIFE, DECLINE, AND THE POWER VACUUM

In the annals of organized crime, the Magaddino Family carved a powerful name for themselves, becoming the name people thought of when thinking about the Buffalo Crime Family. Their reign, however, would not last. The landscape of the criminal underworld was decisively altered in the wake of the infamous Apalachin Meeting. These changes weren't just coming from external rumblings either; they were echoing through the very core of the Magaddino family.

The aging leader of the organization found himself struggling to keep up with such large shifts. The once iron grip of Stefano Magaddino had started to slip away, strained further by the weight of rapidly evolving dynamics. Dissent was bubbling, and like many other families and regimes before, the call for change was becoming harder to ignore.

The twilight of the Magaddino era was riddled with complications, leaving the family staring at the potential for a power vacuum. The eventual death of the Magaddino patriarch would throw the entire organization into uncertainty and turmoil. This chapter serves as a look into the tumultuous last years of the Magaddino Crime Family, exploring those struggles for power, the changes in organized crime as a whole, Stefano's decline, and the absence of any leadership after Stefano's death.

Internal Conflicts and Power Struggles

The Magaddino family was a formidable force in the American Mafia landscape, but they were not immune to power struggles and other internal conflicts. Lower-level thugs and underbosses all had their own ambitions and visions for where they saw the family heading in the future. While unclear as to how many attempts there were to push Stefano off his throne, power struggles commonly led to assassination attempts. This led to more broken leadership and less loyalty within the family, and it would only grow after the failed Apalachin Meeting because of Stefano's ties to its downfall. As time passed by, these pushes were handled with less discipline, which served as a tell-tale sign of the external threats that the family was also facing.

Internal conflicts weren't just unique to the Buffalo Crime Family either. Many other families had the same internal strife as seen in the battles within the Five Families of New York. Some other families, like the Bonanno and Colombo families, experienced them as the landscape was changing from the 1930s to the 1960s. For example, the Bonanno family faced some of their most significant conflicts in the 1960s after Joseph Bonanno mysteriously disappeared. His disappearance led to more power struggles (more than what the families were accustomed to) and a period of instability and violence, as various factions within the family all looked to gain control.

As for the Colombo family, the power struggle began when Carmine Persico, who led the family for decades, was finally imprisoned for his criminal activities. His son Alphonse served as the boss, but without Carmine, his leadership was challenged immediately by other members of the family.

These internal conflicts were typically caused by disagreements over the distribution of power and resources within the family. One of the most notorious examples was the rise of John Gotti in the Gambino family. His ascension led to high tensions and several betrayals until Gotti was imprisoned.

Things were changing rapidly for the American Mafia, and it seemed to happen much faster during the height of the Cold War. Interestingly enough, these power struggles and conflicts seemed to occur at a much faster pace in other families than in the Magaddino family. A lot of this resilience could be attributed to the leadership style of Stefano Magaddino, who managed to keep a certain level of discipline within his family. Again, things wouldn't last as proven by the prominent Bonanno family. Their internal conflict, known as the "Banana War," proved that everything was about to change.

As time went by, the normal iron-fist discipline in the Magaddino family waned and the power struggles only increased.

Attempts on Stefano Magaddino's Life

Where there is smoke, there is fire, and when there are internal conflicts in a Mafia family, that fire is usually in the form of assassination attempts. While Stefano enjoyed a lengthy reign over the Buffalo Crime Family, his life wouldn't be without peril. Assassination attempts were seemingly part of the territory as a crime boss, and Magaddino survived several attempts on his life. Two of those attempts stand out for their sheer audacity and the level of impact that they would have on Stefano and the rest of the family.

1936 Attempt

The first of the most notable attempts on Magaddino's life took place in 1936. While Stefano had been in control of the region for over a decade, others wanted a piece of the lucrative northwestern territory. Skirmishes and hits would break out, but this attempt on Magaddino involved the boss's home and a bomb. However, the plan had one fatal miscalculation. They believed that the bomb was planted in Magaddino's Niagara Falls home, but instead, they planted the bomb in his sister's home. That flaw claimed the life of Stefano's sister and injured his three young nieces.

This incident shook the criminal underworld, but it served as a crucial reminder that the life of a mafioso meant accepting that death lurked around every corner. No one, not even the powerful Magaddino, was immune to spontaneous attacks. The Magaddino organization felt the shockwaves that served as a testament to the collateral damage that came from violence.

The failed assassination was enough to rattle Magaddino, but the loss of his sister had even more of a profound impact on the boss. What followed her murder was a period of intense violence, fueled by his intense desire for revenge against whoever was responsible. Magaddino, known already for his calculated and cautious leadership, had unleashed a wave of retaliation that no one had seen before, as he was determined to also eliminate future threats.

The event marked a turning point for Stefano. While he had previously focused efforts on expanding the Buffalo family's operations, the assassination attempt instilled a heightened sense of paranoia and secrecy. Having something like that hitting so close to home forced him to tighten his grip on the family, which saw him become less trusting and more vigilant.

After Apalachin and the 1958 Attempt

By the time the Apalachin meeting took place, Stefano had been comfortably seated as the boss of the Buffalo crime family for nearly four decades, which was largely because he was a man with ambition who took calculated risks. It was his leadership skills that saw him play a pivotal role in where the large meeting of crime bosses was to take place. While he did have good intentions in mind to use the secluded location to evade the eyes of the law, the plan was a monumental failure. It was his miscalculation that exposed the entirety of the American Mafia network to the public. This brought unwanted attention that would have severe consequences for Magaddino.

In the aftermath of the Apalachin fiasco, there was an instant uptick in the number of assassination attempts made on Stefano. Those bosses who took the fall that day wanted their revenge, and violence was the answer. That violence would reach its boiling point when an assailant threw a hand grenade through the open kitchen window of Magaddino's home. Although the attacker had the right residence this time, fate stepped in. The grenade, a seemingly effective device to take out the Buffalo boss, was a dud. There was no detonation, and Magaddino was safe.

This near-death experience would establish Magaddino as a "Teflon Don," which was a moniker given to those who seemed to never go away. Despite the attempts from rivals and very powerful Mafia bosses, he remained unscathed. His leadership was untouchable, but the attack brought more than a stroke of luck for Stefano. It was a catalyst that spurred another period of ruthless aggression from the boss.

With the kindling of betrayal fueling the attacks, Magaddino grew even more paranoid after this attempt, and he used it to purge several members of the Magaddino Family. Not only was he suspicious of those who may have tipped off the other dons, but he was going for anyone he thought was after his position. Loyalty was the biggest concern, and if Stefano thought anyone was the slightest bit disloyal, they were removed from more than the organization.

The purge did serve Magaddino's other motives. He not only got to eliminate those he felt were disloyal but also potential threats that allowed him to consolidate his power. By weeding out those that he felt were traitors, he looked to prevent any further attempts while establishing himself as an unchallenged boss. He seemed untouchable, but this was only established by instilling fear into those around him.

The Apalachin fiasco was a huge turning point for Magaddino, and things wouldn't be the same during the rest of his time as boss. His remaining years would be a constant struggle, which inadvertently weakened the very thing he tried to fortify.

The Rise in Drug Trafficking and the Heroin Trade

Drug trafficking wasn't anything new to the Mafia, especially as this had been another lucrative venture for many families after the end of Prohibition. However, there would be one product in particular that impacted the power balances within the families, including the Magaddino family. That drug would be heroin, and it offered a huge opportunity for younger mafiosos and underbosses who were eager to gain more wealth and influence.

Again, it would be the younger members of the mafia who were instrumental in pushing for the involvement of heroin in their established trafficking. They saw large financial gains in this venture, and they often overlooked the tremendous risks that were associated with it. This was a slight contrast to the older leaders and underbosses who were a bit more conservative and hesitant. They understood the potential profits, but they also were wary about being associated with the highly addictive substance. This internal strife showed that newer members of the mafia could see the profits while the older family members saw the potential risks, with some being completely against the operation.

One example of this was the Lucchese Family. They were heavily involved in the heroin trade during the 1970s and the 1980s, which was largely driven by the younger members and underbosses. Older leaders were fearful of the increased scrutiny and backlash from the authorities, especially when their operations were going through another major shift and loss of power. The younger members, however, were willing to take the big risk for a bigger reward.

The Bonanno Family's "Banana War" and the power struggle within the family were also largely fueled by disagreements over involvement in the heroin trade. The Magaddinos were not immune to this shift in power and criminal activity either. It was a period of instability, and the drug trafficking racket would only make it worse. Things would also get worse in 1971 when then-President Nixon declared the War on Drugs.

Law Enforcement Efforts

The landscape of the American Mafia was shifting at a rapid rate, and the once dominant crime families across the United States started to lose their grip on the territories they controlled. But it wasn't just the dynamic shifts within the family; organizations lost their once powerful hold on law enforcement and the court system as well. Naturally, this would mean the same for Stefano and the Magaddino family.

Law enforcement, from local and state to federal agencies, was also in a seismic shift. Fearful of how the public would react to their complacency after the Mafia was exposed, they ramped up their efforts to take down the crime families. The Magaddino Family was no exception, with an increased focus on the infiltration and disruption of criminal activities. The number of informants increased exponentially during this period. While some informants were officers, many of these came from within the organization itself. With ambitions to move up or fear of punishment by the law, family members gave up valuable information. The insider knowledge of family activities gave law enforcement valuable insight, which allowed them to make more effective strikes to disrupt the family's operations.

Informant information led to a series of effective raids and arrests, and these actions dealt major blows to various operations. This disrupted activities and led to the arrest (and conviction) of lower-level thugs and underbosses. Once extensive and robust networks were either damaged or severed completely. The loss of key personnel and a large number of members quickly and significantly reduced the power and influence the crime family held over the regions.

The rest of the legal system would follow suit, as legal cases against the family significantly increased. Prosecutors were armed with a mountain of evidence thanks to various informants and the evidence gathered during raids. Strong cases were made against the defendants, which often resulted in long prison sentences, depleting the family's ranks.

The most notable of these moves from law enforcement was the Apalachin Meeting. Again, the suspicious activity led law enforcement to the conclusion that this was criminal activity. Many Mafia bosses were arrested, and while there was a relatively minor impact on the Magaddino Family, some of Magaddino's underbosses did go down in the raid. The most significant aspect of the raid was that law enforcement was no longer going to sit idly by and let the Mafia continue their operations.

Loss of Influence and Territory

The Magaddinos were no doubt a resilient force, but they began to experience a decline in their territory because of the internal and external factors that have been mentioned.

Internally, the family was trying to navigate through the fallout in the wake of the assassination attempts on Stefano. This led to a period of instability within the family, with members questioning each other and their loyalty to the Magaddino organization. With the constant threat of violence and fear of retaliation, a tense atmosphere spread across the family and impeded the smooth operation of their activities.

Externally, the decline of the Magaddino reign was spurred by public outcry and the sudden shift in how law enforcement handled the Mafia. With efforts now ramped up to combat organized crime, a sense of further distrust and paranoia was taking root in the family. While the consolidation of power would cut down on these betrayals, it would be a double-edged sword, as the family would find their grip loosening on the region.

Despite the contributions made to the local economy through their enterprises and philanthropy, the Magaddinos weren't protected. The call for justice against the American Mafia was spreading, which led to either rebranding or the shedding of some businesses to keep the heat off.

As the influence of the Magaddino Family waned, the door for rivals and other criminal organizations to capitalize on the territory opened. The groups moved in and attempted to take over. The family couldn't retaliate like they would have done, further weakening them and accelerating their loss of power.

The Final Years of the Magaddino Family

In the year following the Apalachin Meeting, the writing was on the wall that the Magaddino Crime Family would enter a period of great decline. The FBI gave Stefano the label of "top hoodlum" in the Buffalo region. This label was put in place by FBI Director Hoover, and it would come with heavy scrutiny from law enforcement. While the FBI had the boss under heavy surveillance, Magaddino managed to avoid questioning related to the Apalachin Meeting by the New York State Crime Commission in 1960 because he fell ill with a heart condition. Magaddino avoided dire consequences for his involvement in the meeting, but the authorities would not give up there.

In 1961, American *and* Canadian authorities would tear apart a narcotics ring that had Magaddino's approval. This was a strong point for the family, and Stefano took a share of the profits. It could have also been his undoing though.

Among the persons arrested were Alberto and Vito Agueci. The brothers were Magaddino underlings from Canada, and after their arrest, they expected protection and support from their boss. However, Stefano left them high and dry. Alberto was eventually freed on bail thanks to his wife borrowing money and selling their family home. His plan after release was to confront the Buffalo crime boss and demand the release of his brother. Furthermore, he planned on putting the squeeze on Stefano. Alberto would threaten to expose Magaddino's involvement in the drug ring if Vito wasn't released.

While not confirmed, Stefano likely didn't take kindly to the threat because, on November 23, 1961, Alberto's charred body was found in a cornfield near Rochester.

In 1962, the FBI would install eavesdropping equipment in the heart of the Magaddino empire. The Magaddino Memorial Chapel, which served as the meeting place for Stefano and his underbosses, was bugged. The equipment would gather enough damning information in less than three years, enough for the FBI to fill around 70,000 transcribed pages. There was even enough that in 1963, in front of the McClellan Senate Investigating Committee, Stefano Magaddino was identified as the Mafia boss of western New York and southern Ontario, Canada.

In 1964, after the disappearance of Joseph Bonanno, who was Magaddino's cousin, a newspaper columnist put out a report stating that Bonanno was being held by Magaddino in upstate New York. Stefano was subpoenaed in May 1965 to give his testimony to a special grand jury that was looking into Bonanno's disappearance. However, Magaddino, once again, didn't say a word as he developed coronary symptoms the very next day. He was hospitalized and wouldn't testify. It didn't go unnoticed though, as the press made sure to note that this was the second time that Magaddino's "health problems" seemed to go hand in hand with a government demand for him to testify.

Things from the government's side would ramp up in 1967, and federal law enforcement launched strikes against the western New York Mafia's leadership. By December of that year, Magaddino lost Frederico Randaccio and Pasquale Natarelli (two of his top-ranking men) to prison sentences. Magaddino would quickly unravel under the pressure. He claimed that he was reaching poverty, so he demanded a higher share of family profits. Stefano also eliminated bonuses that had been previously handed out.

That move would be exposed a year later when Stefano, his son Peter, and several bookmakers and collectors were arrested after the

FBI investigated a Buffalo sports betting ring. When federal agents searched Peter Magaddino's home, they found over $500,000 in cash. Leaders within the Buffalo Mafia were enraged that Stefano had lied to them about his finances, and a rebellion against the Magaddino administration was ignited.

By mid-year 1969, a rebel faction formed, with Sam Pieri as acting boss, Joseph Fino as acting underboss, and Joseph DiCarlo (son of Giuseppe) as consigliere. The group demanded that Stefano resign his position, which was refused. They then took their argument to the Commission, but the Commission took no action against the longtime member. They chose to await the death of the aging Magaddino.

It wasn't what the rebel faction wanted, but Stefano's time was coming quickly. His health problems made it nearly impossible to bring the long-reigning boss to trial. His arraignment in the bookmaking case was done in Magaddino's bedrooms when doctors deemed him too frail to appear in a courtroom. Despite his frailty, Stefano would slip through the fingers of the law one last time. In 1973, the FBI, having Magaddino dead to rights, refused to give up the identity of one of their informants who had been a part of the bookmaking investigation. Without that identity, the charges that Magaddino faced were dismissed.

Stefano "The Undertaker" Magaddino, a true Teflon Don, suffered a heart attack and died on July 19, 1974. He was buried in St. Joseph's Cemetery in Niagara Falls, where he had spent the better part of five decades as the face of the Mafia in the northwest part of New York.

The Power Vacuum and Power Struggles

Stefano Magaddino's death would leave a very noticeable hole in the leadership of the family. The once-powerful organization, which had already been weakened because of internal conflict, was now plunged into a period of instability. Several factions that sprang up in Magaddino's last days were all focused on power and control, which led to much more infighting. This internal drama left the Buffalo family fractured, desperate, and quickly losing precious territory.

The path to leadership wasn't clear either. Peter Magaddino, Stefano's son, looked to be the heir apparent to his father's position. However, he would step aside and leave the family after his involvement in his father's shady practices.

Sam Pieri, the leader of the faction that challenged Magaddino's authority the most in the years before his death, emerged as the strongest candidate. He did take the reins, giving some semblance of stability. However, that wouldn't last long, as Pieri's reign was short-lived. In 1978, he was hit with a prison sentence, which left the leadership role wide open yet again.

The Buffalo family was struggling to stay afloat. They needed a leader who could command respect the way that DiCarlo and Magaddino did. They needed someone ruthless to navigate them back to prominence, and they needed someone to navigate through one of the biggest shifts in the Mafia. The 1980s changed the landscape and threatened to snuff out the dim flame that was the Buffalo Crime Family.

PART III
THE TODARO FAMILY
(1980S-2020S-PRESENT)

CHAPTER 6
THE STATE OF THE MAFIA IN THE 1980S

The 1980s saw a major turning point in the American underworld. The vice grip that the Mafia had over their territories began to loosen, and its aging leadership had to come to terms with the perfect combination of internal and external pressures. The older leaders were either retiring, succumbing to old age, or finding themselves behind iron bars due to the increased pressure from law enforcement. Power vacuums were created in the absence of leaders, which would be true when looking at the disarray the Buffalo Crime Family was left in after Magaddino's death. Territories were shrinking every day and operations were under heavy scrutiny from the law. Moreover, there was a vast shift in the public perception of the Mafia. What had been one of the most powerful forces in the underworld was now struggling to hold on to some semblance of power.

When they weren't struggling with internal conflicts and external pressures, the families were trying to find new ways to maintain a steady flow of revenue. Traditional operations like gambling, racketeering, and loan sharking were still around, but they weren't nearly as profitable as they had once been. The new cash cow was narcotics trafficking, but that would come with its own heavy price in the form of increased attention from law enforcement. With a surge in arrests and convictions, the already rocky landscape was even more difficult to navigate.

Adding to the woes was the newfound fascination the media had with the criminal underworld. Gangster films like *The Godfather* and *Scarface*, television shows, and even news reports seemed to put more focus on the sensational aspects of the media. This not only skewed public perception, but it also potentially attracted newer members to the Mafia under the pretense of a lavish life.

Despite the changes, the American Mafia would still be able to hold a significant presence in the criminal underworld. However, their influence had waned. The late 1970s and the 1980s would be a crucial turning point that would see the once dominant American Mafia struggle to hang on to their influence. This chapter will look at the Mafia's struggle to adapt to an era defined by pressure from law enforcement, infighting, shifting public opinion, and the impact of the media.

The Changing Landscape of Organized Crime

The glamorous, powerful portrayal of the American Mafia in popular culture was a far cry from reality. What was fed to the general masses was a portrayal of an organization with a strict code of honor, with a refusal to get involved in drug trafficking because of the morality behind it. While there were some factions and older leaders that resisted, it was something that many would look past after they saw the allure of immense profits. Increased revenue amid shrinking territories that were under Mafia control was something they couldn't resist. This was certainly the case in the Buffalo Crime

Family's involvement in the drug trade under the leadership of Stefano Magaddino and eventually Joseph Todaro Sr. It also kept the family alive during the power vacuum that was created after Stefano's death.

Again, the choice to move into the narcotics trade wasn't driven by any sense of morality or lack thereof. It was driven by cold, hard economics. Traditional Mafia operations like gambling, racketeering, and loan sharking were losing their luster. However, the drug trade was booming, especially as the war on drugs actually increased the demand. However, the move toward drugs came with its own share of consequences. Mafia families found themselves in the middle of some violent turf wars, not just with rival families but also with a new breed of criminal organizations. Immigrant gangs from other places besides Sicily were spreading out, and there was also a rise in homegrown criminal outfits of various backgrounds. Everyone was looking for a piece of the pie, which led to increased conflict and resulted in a boon for law enforcement—the same law enforcement that had gained a wealth of resources to combat the escalating war on drugs. Therefore, every turf war and every drop of blood was open season for police scrutiny.

The move into narcotics would also deal a tremendous blow to the Mafia's already tarnished image. The impact that drugs had on communities and specific demographics was far more visible and destructive than anything that the Mafia had been tied to before. There was no longer an "invisible hand" that guided the underworld activity. It was now a very visible, destructive force, much like the very street gangs that the Mafia had once looked down upon.

For the Buffalo Crime Family, navigating through this shift was particularly difficult. After Magaddino died, he left behind no successor. So, while the rebel faction that rose against him took his position, there were increased internal conflicts. The organization was now caught between wanting to hang on to the traditions of the past and having to face the harsh realities that were tied to the world of drugs. This internal pressure, in conjunction with the external pressure from law enforcement and turf wars, threw the Buffalo family into further disarray. That itself led to further consequences, beyond internal strife and bad reputations. Violence had now taken control of the communities that they tried so hard to control.

The landscape was certainly not like the romanticized image that a lot of people had, and no one felt that more than the people who were still living in Mafia territory.

Increased Law Enforcement Efforts

The battle against the American Mafia wasn't a new phenomenon and had been going on well before the 1960s. The disaster known as the Apalachin Meeting in 1957 exposed the entire Mafia network in the United States. This raid by law enforcement served as a reminder that no one would be above the law forever and of the Mafia's growing vulnerability. However, the late 1970s and the 1980s would see a significant rise in efforts by law enforcement agencies across the country. Every Mafia family, including the once-powerful Buffalo family, was beginning to feel the squeeze.

This era saw a huge increase in not only awareness of Mafia activities but also a much more aggressive response from both federal agencies and local authorities. The Racketeer Influenced and

Corrupt Organizations (RICO) Act, passed in 1970, would be a game-changer for those agencies. It gave law enforcement more resources and powerful legal tools to go after and dismantle organized crime. RICO wasn't an act that would hand out more fines or short jail sentences; it was aimed to send mafiosos away for long stints in prison. They were also out to seize any assets acquired through illegal activities. Furthermore, the act let those agencies offer incentives for Mafia members (no matter their rank) to become witnesses of the state. Organizations would be weakened from within by encouraging betrayals of underbosses and other high-ranking members.

One of the most significant effects of this increased offensive was felt in Las Vegas, the city that was built on the back of the Mafia. For years, Sin City had been a lucrative hotspot that was very much under Mafia control. However, the FBI and local police forces teamed up and began to crack down on the Mafia. They used carefully planned efforts to take control of the casinos away from the embrace of the underworld. This move went hand-in-hand with efforts that would take Mafia influence out of the labor unions, which had been another significant source of revenue and power for the families. Buffalo and many other cities where the Mafia held significant power would feel the impact head-on.

These actions occurred toward the end of Stefano's reign, while there were internal struggles ignited by his deception. The organization couldn't escape the pressure, and again, Stefano himself faced two separate subpoenas and narrowly avoided imprisonment several times thanks to some well-timed illnesses. However, several key figures within the Magaddino family had fallen because of the increased scrutiny by law enforcement. This only made things more difficult for the family after Magaddino died. Even when Joseph Todaro Sr. took over, he had to deal with a weakened family while operating in an environment that was growing increasingly hostile.

Of course, despite the challenges, the Mafia wouldn't fully succumb to extinction. However, their power was significantly diminished. The aggression shown by law enforcement during these crucial years marked a turning point, and the once-untouchable Mafia now had to contend with a coordinated, supported, and well-resourced enemy. It was a far cry from the empire that had smuggled alcohol while the law turned a blind eye.

The Changing Dynamics Within the Mafia

By 1974, the cracks had already appeared in the decades-old foundation of the Magaddino Crime Family. Stefano, who had been the dominant leader, was facing dissent from outside of the family, especially after Apalachin. He also faced growing dissent within his own organization in the wake of his shady practices. Despite the loss of respect for the Buffalo boss in his final years, his death would still trigger a rough patch that led the family through even more chaos.

Magaddino's passing would cause a noticeable power vacuum. Underbosses and other members saw this as their opportunity to seize control, which ignited a ruthless internal war. It started as an attempt to gain influence to elevate their status; however, that boiled over into an open conflict. Factions, like the one that tried to remove Magaddino from his position, formed. The loyalties of these factions, however, were fueled by personal gain and long-standing grievances instead of the overall stability of the family. Eventually, the battles would be felt on the streets of Buffalo, mirroring the overall changing landscape of the Mafia.

The internal strife in the Buffalo organization wasn't an isolated phenomenon, as the 1980s bore witness to a surge of violence across the world of organized crime. America and Sicily saw body counts rise exponentially as rival families and inner factions clashed for control of operations and territory. While numerous events throughout their history shaped the direction of the Mafia, the 1980s would see its character significantly altered.

Despite the internal conflict, the Buffalo family would still hold onto some control in northwest New York. However, the influence that they had at this time paled in comparison to what it had been during the height of Magaddino's reign. The family was fractured, with unity being replaced by the struggle for leadership. There was now a level of uncertainty hanging in the air.

This period of instability would last for several years after 1974. There wouldn't be a period of calm until a formidable successor was chosen, which would be in the form of Joseph Todaro Sr. He would be the one to finally reconsolidate the family's power. It would be through his cunning strategy and ruthlessness that much of the infighting would stop and the family would be ushered into a new era.

However, the scars of these battles would linger throughout the Mafia. While the Buffalo family regained their grip on the region, they wouldn't be able to return to their former glory.

The Impact of Public Perception and Media

In the 1980s, there was another shift regarding the Mafia, and it was in the form of a public fascination that was continuously rising. This was no coincidence either. It was fueled by media coverage that transformed a once-secretive organization into a staple in pop culture. News reports, books, films, and television shows thrived on exposing the criminal underworld and their violence, rituals, and iconic leaders. While these expositions shed light on the illegal aspects of their operations, the Mafia was often glorified, even in news reports. Their lifestyle was seen by the public as glamorous and powerful. What the general population saw was a fictionalized image, which was a far cry from the brutal reality that those living in Mafia-controlled areas experienced.

The Buffalo family wasn't an exception to this trend. The real-world activities of extortion, loan sharking, gambling rackets, drug trafficking, and murder were just as sensationalized during this period. While the region wasn't as prominent as some of the more notorious regions, there was still a public eye on the family because of their involvement with the American Mafia. It only solidified their notorious reputation, but the focus on sensationalism came at a cost.

The fascination the media had with the flashier aspects like expensive suits, luxury cars, and lavish lifestyles never highlighted the destructive impact the Mafia had on individuals, businesses, and communities. Often left out of the narratives were the fear, intimidation, and violent tendencies that would drive operations. These were either downplayed or turned into elements of respect or a last resort (using violence because there was no other option).

Matters were also not helped thanks to films like *Scarface* and *The Godfather*. While mobster movies had existed since the 1930s, films like this rose in popularity during this time and contributed to the swaying of public perception. They would present the dramatized family dynamic while showing power, ruthlessness, and a strict code of honor.

Unless one was in proximity to Mafia-controlled regions, the embellished portrayal didn't just distort the truth but also put distance between people and the reality of the Mafia's influence. They included stylized violence, romanticized operations, and consequences that only felt like they existed in the mob world. When it all looked like a thrilling story, it was hard to see it as a dangerous reality.

With that said, even in the media frenzy of the 1980s, there were attempts to establish the actual narrative. Documentaries and investigative pieces attempted to shed light on the reality of Mafia life. These exposés were less prevalent and usually less popular, but they did offer a much-needed counterpoint to other portrayals.

The 1980s would shape a new perception of the Mafia, and it would only grow over time. While there were still popular characters on the fictional side of things, there were also reality shows based on families with Mafia ties. Furthermore, there were several books, podcasts, and other pieces that fueled interest in the Mafia. However, as the years have passed, many of these media pieces show the harsh reality of the Mafia. They shed light on the law enforcement agencies who are out to stop organized crime, and they also expose the very harsh realities of what life is really like within the mob.

A New Leader on the Rise

The 1980s proved to be a rough patch for the American Mafia. Power struggles only intensified as new leadership tried to push beyond the traditions set generations before. The Buffalo Crime Family, which had been mired in conflict (both internal and external), found itself especially vulnerable during this time.

The death of Stefano Magaddino left a void in the organization that was felt for years. Factions within the family, all hungry for ultimate power, clashed, fracturing what had been one of the quietest, most powerful families in New York. The streets of Buffalo and Niagara Falls became a battleground that mirrored the worldwide decline of the Mafia. A sense of desperation now hung over the region.

The Buffalo family severely needed a force to unify it again, a leader who was cunning and ruthless and wouldn't be afraid to navigate this new landscape. That leader was steadily rising up the ranks, and in the tumultuous atmosphere, Joseph Todaro Sr. emerged. He was the cunning individual who presented answers to the questions that had been lingering in the organization. But one very crucial question would arise with Todaro's ascension: Could he, amidst the instability, restore the once prominent Buffalo family to the glory they had been accustomed to? Only time, and Todaro's leadership skills, would tell.

CHAPTER 7

JOSEPH "PAPA JOE" TODARO SR.

In the history of organized crime, the Buffalo Crime Family long stood as a testament to the incredible dynamics of power and leadership. Yet after Stefano Magaddino's death, there was a scramble for control within the notorious family. That scramble would last nearly a decade, which proved to be enough time to establish a sense of uncertainty and instability in the organization.

Various figures would step up to fill the vacant seat. While each of them brought a unique approach and vision for the family, none of them could encapsulate the complex role of a leader, especially the leader of a criminal organization. That role did not ask for respect; it demanded it. A leader like this would need that, along with a cunning nature and an iron resolve.

This sticky situation was something the Buffalo family had never experienced to this point. The family's solid foundation was led by the short yet effective reign of DiCarlo and Palmeri. They established Buffalo's roots in the underworld and following them was the incredible reign of Stefano Magaddino. He took the helm and built on that foundation, guiding the organization to incredible levels of power and influence.

The world was changing for the Mafia, and the Buffalo family was standing at a crossroads. Everything that its previous leaders had accomplished was in danger of being lost to time, which meant that the family needed to change course. The need for a leader to get them through this tumultuous time was at its highest.

Enter Joseph Todaro Sr., a name that now resonates with power and influence in the history books of organized crime. Todaro's life in and out of the Mafia was one of controversy and intrigue, but he was just the man who could breathe new life into an organization that needed it. His leadership would mark a turning point for the Buffalo Crime Family, rejuvenating their operations and re-establishing its place in the criminal underworld.

This chapter dives into the rise of Joseph Todaro Sr., exploring his journey up to becoming the chosen leader of the Buffalo Crime Family. It will examine how he navigated the dynamics of power, stayed ahead of his rivals, and ensured that the family, now known as the Todaro family, would survive in the rapidly changing landscape.

The Early Years of Todaro

Joseph Todaro was born on September 18, 1923, to Anthony Todaro and Sarah Frangiamore. Call it "right place, right time" because Joe's life was deeply intertwined into the webs of organized crime.

Joe would later marry Josephine Santamauro, and the couple would have three children: Carol, Joseph Jr. who would follow in his father's footsteps into a life of crime, and Linda who would later marry Peter Gerace who was also involved in the Buffalo crime world.

Given the name "Lead Pipe Joe," and sometimes "Papa Joe," by his associates in crime, Todaro Sr. held the position of caporegime in the Buffalo family. This was a role that carried a lot of significance within the Mafia hierarchy, and it put him in charge of his own crew of soldiers. So, very early on, Todaro already had influence and control within the organization. As Joseph Todaro Jr. got older, he along with Papa Joe and his uncle Richard Todaro would control the family's bookmaking operations, which was still a very lucrative gambling racket.

By the early 1960s, after the infamous Apalachin meeting, Stefano Magaddino had started to delegate a lot of the daily activities of the family to one of his underbosses, Frederico Randaccio. While Stefano was still at the head of the table, Randaccio's assumption of power would mark the change in the Magaddino family and their dynamics. Randaccio's operations ran out of the Blue Banner Social Club during the 1960s and 1970s. That club, controlled by a Buffalo family soldier, Benny Spano, was a hub for a lot of the family's activities during this time, including the activities of Todaro Sr.

Todaro Sr. rightfully earned his position within the family as he was a significant money-maker for the Magaddino family. This would lead him to take part in more rackets, including card and dice games, loansharking, Las Vegas junkets, and even labor rackets. These activities brought in substantial profits for the family, which helped boost their financial power and influence in the underworld. A large portion of this could be attributed to Todaro's work; however, during those tumultuous years when Magaddino was taking money for himself, there wasn't much that Papa Joe could do.

Todaro Sr. didn't work without risks though, which was just part of life in the underworld. In May 1967, Todaro Sr. and 35 men were arrested at a party. The charge against Papa Joe was "consorting with known criminals," which was a very serious accusation that could have done a lot of damage to his operations and his reputation. Yet, Todaro, like the bosses before him, had a stroke of luck as the charges were dismissed in court, which allowed him to continue his activities unscathed.

Later, on the night of March 13, 1982, Papa Joe was in the middle of a huge brawl outside of the Buffalo Playboy Club. Not only was he caught in the violence, but he was an active participant, stepping in to help out Daniel Sansanese Jr. While he had been great at keeping his head down, the brawl was simply a reminder of how volatile and violent the criminal world was.

The Playboy Club is important here because FBI logs concerning Todaro Sr. revealed how skilled the caporegime was at conducting mob business away from attention. Papa Joe held meetings in hotel rooms and VIP rooms around the area. This kept prying eyes away, but it also added an air of exclusivity and secrecy around his businesses. His preferred venues, however, were the Executive Inn, the 747s disco, and the Playboy Club. These establishments, which were dotted conveniently around the Greater Buffalo International Airport in Cheektowaga, New York, all gave Todaro the perfect cover. Therefore, the brawl was actually one of the first big signs that something much bigger was happening behind the closed doors of the club.

From Caporegime to Boss

Again, there was no one to take up the mantle in Buffalo who could recapture even a bit of what the family had been in the past. However, the significant change that the family needed would come in 1984. Samuel Frangiamore, the man who took on the role of boss, decided to step down from the position. His retirement paved the way for Joseph Todaro Sr., who had been a hotshot caporegime, to transcend his previous role and become head of the Buffalo Crime Family. One of his first orders of business was to appoint his son, Joseph Todaro Jr. as one of his new underbosses, which marked the beginning of the Todaro Family.

1984-1990

Things had so far been working for Papa Joe, but his leadership would soon be put to the test. In 1985, not even a year after assuming the position, he was charged with federal tax evasion. Todaro Sr. had come under fire for underreporting his income for three years (1976, 1977, and 1978). These were severe charges, and they could have jeopardized the future of the Buffalo organization, but Joe Sr. managed to carefully navigate the legal proceedings. He would eventually be acquitted, and this matter would be the first example of his resilience and ability to endure anything that came his way. It was a welcome sign for the Buffalo family.

Things may have taken on an old familiar feeling of the bygone days of the Magaddino Crime Family, but this was a new landscape, and the authorities were consistently putting pressure on criminal organizations, which meant that Todaro would also be dealing with them while trying to re-solidify the Buffalo territory.

The pressure came on Todaro Sr. again in 1989 when the FBI filed a statement in connection with an investigation they were carrying out into gambling rings. The federal agency named Todaro Sr. and Todaro Jr. as leading figures of the Buffalo Mafia. This statement also named 45 made members of the organization. It was no longer a rumor, as the family was reported to control several criminal activities in the area, including labor racketeering, bookmaking, loansharking, and drug trafficking. This would also be one of the first times that Todaro Jr. would be named the boss of the family by federal agents. The statements in this investigation said that Jr. was running the family on behalf of Papa Joe, who had semi-retired from the criminal underworld, spending his time between his properties in Florida and New York.

That same investigation in 1989 also revealed that Leonard F. Falzone, a member of the Laborers' International Union of North America Local 210, was operating a loansharking operation for the Todaro Family. Also named were brothers Victor and Daniel Sansanese, who were members of Local 210. The brothers were reportedly in control of a bookmaking operation for the Todaros.

In the year before this FBI statement came to light, federal agents had bugged Falzone's union-owned car in an attempt to try and link the Todaros to the illegal gambling case. However, the bug failed to get agents the evidence they needed, which was more than a lucky break for the Todaros.

Despite the initial setback for the FBI, the bug planted in Falzone's car would also be a huge break for the authorities. The information taken from that surveillance operation gave them more than enough evidence to take down the Torina drug ring, a notorious operation that was responsible for millions of dollars in street sales of cocaine annually in the city of Buffalo. It would mark a significant victory for law enforcement agencies like the DEA and the FBI, who had been working tirelessly to find some sort of crack in the foundation of the criminal underworld.

As their investigation continued into the Torina drug ring, it shed light on the involvement of Papa Joe Todaro and Leonard Falzone in a Las Vegas-to-Buffalo pipeline for cocaine and other illegal operations. The revelation was huge as it exposed the extent of Mafia influence and just how far-reaching the Todaro Family operations still were, spanning across state lines and involving a complex web of illegal activities.

That investigation would come to fruition on March 20, 1990, when Mafia operations suffered a huge blow. Las Vegas police arrested Louis Giambrone, Joseph Amoia, and Lawrence Panero, who were all Buffalo natives and named as members of the Buffalo Crime Family. That alone was enough to tighten law enforcement's grip over the family's activities, but there would be more to it. Charles Torina, another Buffalo native, was identified as a key link in this drug pipeline from Las Vegas to Buffalo. Torina, who had previously worked as a pit boss in a Las Vegas casino, was now wrapped up in the Todaro Family's activities.

These events marked a turning point in the long-standing fight against organized crime, especially as fewer and fewer authorities were complicit in what was happening around them. This highlighted their new perspective and their relentless efforts to infiltrate and cause irrefutable damage to the Buffalo Crime Family and others like them. At the same time, however, this showed the resiliency and adaptability of Papa Joe. He continued to navigate the rougher waters of this criminal landscape, which showed that he was the right man for the job.

This wouldn't be the Todaro family's only brush with the law that year. Canadian police had conducted a large operation of their own, which resulted in the arrest of 14 suspects connected to a drug ring. As they learned more about these individuals, they unveiled deep-rooted connections to the organized crime units running out of Buffalo and Niagara Falls.

An anonymous agent tied to the investigation would also reveal that any activity in St. Catharines, Hamilton, Niagara Falls, and any surrounding communities required the approval of the Buffalo (Todaro) Crime Family, which further revealed the extent of their influence. This was the control established by DiCarlo, solidified by Magaddino, and resurrected by Todaro. Every mob family in the region answered to Buffalo.

Among those who were arrested were associates of John Anticoli. Anticoli was a businessman from Niagara Falls who, at the time, was serving a 10-year sentence in federal prison. Anticoli was a huge part of the Todaro network and was described by the FBI as one of the most significant drug dealers that had ever been apprehended in western New York. He would plead guilty to several of the charges brought on him, which included the possession of 270 pounds of marijuana, conspiracy to distribute cocaine, tax evasion, and failure to pay taxes on his drug profits.

Also, some of those arrested were Carmen Barillaro, Nicodemo Bruzzese, and Dominic Vaccaro, who were identified as "made men" of a crime family based in Hamilton, Ontario, which was operating under the indirect control of the Buffalo mob. This was even more proof for the FBI that the influence of the Todaro family was still just as wide as it had been under the leadership of Magaddino. However, the operation itself would be a significant step in the fight against organized crime that was happening across the nation.

The 1990s

Besides the two key breaks for federal agents against the Buffalo Crime Family, the Todaro family continued to grow. On September 6, 1993, Joseph Todaro III, married Dana Christine Panepinto, the daughter of Donald Panepinto, who had a large hand in Local 210, further extending the family's connections and influence into the labor unions of the area.

Things would ease a bit for the Todaro family, but calm waters wouldn't last. By 1996, the organization found itself under scrutiny yet again. Joseph Todaro Sr. and Joseph Todaro Jr. were listed with 24 other organized crime figures. All 24 figures were accused of having influence in the Laborers International Union of North America since the 1960s. The accusations only shed more light on the family's long-standing involvement in labor racketeering, which put the most lucrative and powerful portion of organized crime in jeopardy.

Despite yet another challenge placed before them, the Todaro family's operations would expand beyond Buffalo. Carmen Milano, an underboss of a Los Angeles crime outfit, reached out to Papa Joe about potentially joining forces. Together, the two organizations would take over a loan sharking and auto insurance fraud racket in Las Vegas. The operation's head was slated to be Herbert Blitztein, who was an associate of the Chicago outfit. Milano said that Todaro Sr. would get a piece of the profits that Blitztein's rackets brought in. This was going to be a significant expansion in the family's operations. The Buffalo and Los Angeles families arranged for Robert Panaro, who at the time was a foot soldier in the Buffalo family, to be the receiver for Blitztein's stolen jewelry. Everything seemed to be set on the right track until the entire plan took a dark turn.

On January 6, 1997, Antonio Davi and Richard Friedman, who were associates of the Los Angeles crime family shot and killed Herbert Blitztein in his own home. Peter Caruso, who was simply an associate of the L.A. family, had been behind the hit and took over the Las Vegas operations. The business partnership's operations had dried up, and the year would continue to dole out critical blows on the family.

The next upheaval in 1997 was when Johnny Papalia, the boss of the Buffalo family's Canadian faction, and Carmen Barillaro (Papalia's lieutenant) were assassinated by Kenneth Murdock. It would take nearly two years for federal agents to apprehend Murdock, and when they did, he decided to roll over and become a government witness. He confessed that he carried out the hit ordered by Pasquale "Pat" Musitano and his brother Angelo of the Musitano crew.

Murdock told the government that the brothers were no longer content with just being a "satellite crew" of the Buffalo family and paying them tribute money. Murdock would also reveal that the two assassinations were only the beginning and that he was awaiting the approval of orders to eliminate four members of the Luppino crew, another powerful Mafia family. These revelations shed new light on the complex dynamics and rivalries that were taking place in the new landscape of organized crime. However, as much as the government learned from Murdock, they would also learn a lot more.

Murdock told agents that Pat Musitano discussed with Vito Rizzuto (Quebec Marfia boss) and Gaetano Panepinto about Rizzuto investing money into Ontario. Canadian intelligence agencies had already been on their trail, but investigations ramped up after the double assassination of Papalia and Barillaro. They would go on to observe several meetings between Musitano and Rizzuto. It wouldn't take long before these agencies were convinced that the Musitano brothers were not acting alone in the hits.

In 1998, Lee Coppola, who was a veteran reporter of organized crime for *The Buffalo News*, wrote an article titled "The Withered Arm." In the piece, he discussed how the once-powerful Buffalo Crime Family was now in shambles, disorganized, and essentially broke, which was a far cry from the power and influence the family had during the Magaddino reign. The article also stated that the last bits of mob power had disappeared in Buffalo. It would have looked like the obituary of the Buffalo crime family, but Coppola's article was just a bit premature.

A year after said article, in 1999, Canadian intelligence found that a new crime lord had emerged, and this person was connected to the Todaro family, proving they still had just as much influence despite the setbacks. The figure would remain anonymous to public knowledge, but they had significant control in the region. They were the head of the Golden Horseshoe region of Ontario, which had a strong relationship with outlaw bikers. This was something that his predecessor, Johny Papalia, did not have. The unnamed boss and his new alliances led Peter Polcetti (Detective Sergeant of the CISC) to declare that the family was in firm control over Niagara, Hamilton, Toronto, and Montreal.

In that same year, Papa Joe, his son Joseph Todaro Jr., and 16 other individuals were named in a civil racketeering lawsuit. All 18 were accused of controlling Local 210 with various racketeering operations over the years. The significance of this lawsuit was how it identified Joseph Todaro Sr. as the boss and Joseph Todaro Jr. as the underboss of the Buffalo Crime Family. It also identified the father and son as owners of La Nova Pizzeria. While Papa Joe was never a member of the union, Todaro Jr had served as its business manager in 1990 before he resigned. The family was hard-pressed to work around the charges because they were based on the testimony of Ronald Fino, who had also served as a business manager of Local 210 before becoming an FBI informant.

The Final Years of Papa Joe Todaro

In June 2004, Todaro Sr. would once again find himself in the crosshairs of the law, as he became a person of interest in the unsolved murder of Charles Gerass in 1965. However, despite the serious nature of the accusations made, the investigation led nowhere, and there were no charges against Papa Joe or anyone else.

In 2006, Joseph Todaro Sr. retired as head of the Buffalo Crime Family, passing the role of boss (officially) to his son Joseph Todaro Jr. Leonard Falzone was named the underboss of Todaro Jr., a position that he held until he passed away in 2016.

Throughout his reign, Papa Joe, his son, and the rest of the family faced numerous allegations from local agencies, the FBI, and the US Justice Department. They even came under fire for being the leaders of Buffalo's La Cosa Nostra family, but those allegations were never proven. Therefore, despite the tremendous pressure that the Mafia and the Todaro family faced during his reign, Papa Joe lived his entire life without ever being convicted of a felony crime.

Outside of the organized crime world, Papa Jope was also a successful businessman. He opened La Nova Pizzeria in 1957, a legitimate business that went from a small restaurant to a lucrative business. That business would thrive under one location until a second location of La Nova Pizzeria was opened in Amherst.

Joseph Todaro Sr. would have a lengthy battle with illness and succumb to it on December 26, 2012, at age 89. While he relinquished control six years prior, his death still marked the end of an era for the Buffalo Crime Family.

CHAPTER 8

JOSEPH "BIG JOE" TODARO JR.

While the history of the Buffalo family has always been a tale of power, ambition, and survival; for much of its existence, the leadership of the family wasn't determined by a blood tie. Angelo Palmeri stepped down and handed control over to Giuseppe DiCarlo. Although Joseph DiCarlo was Giuseppe's son, the family was handed over to Stefano Magaddino.

Magaddino was known for his very long reign over the family, and while his son Peter was part of the family, Peter would leave after his father's death. Salvatore "Sam the Farmer" Frangiamore held the family together during that tumultuous period. That transition of power would break the uncertain pattern after the rise of Joseph "Papa Joe" Todaro Sr. His son Joseph "Big Joe" Todaro Jr. was the underboss. This move set Big Joe up to take over the family's leadership after the death of Papa Joe in 2012.

For Big Joe, this chapter will take a step back to give more focus on the eventual leader of the Buffalo Crime Family.

The Early Years

Joseph A. Todaro Jr., later known as "Big Joe" in the Buffalo Crime Family was born in the mid-1940s into the world of power, influence, and illicit activities. He was, of course, the son of Joseph Todaro Sr. and Josephine Santamauro, the former being a key component in the Buffalo family. Big Joe later married Carol Ann, whom he affectionately calls "Cookie." The couple would have two children, Joesph E Todaro III and Carla, the latter would go on to marry Salvatore Pantano, which further cemented the Todaro family's roots within the criminal underworld.

Big Joe didn't have to wait long before following in his father's footsteps. His journey started when he became a business agent for the Laborers' International Union of North America Local 210. It was a position that gave him a legitimate front while also opening up opportunities to extend the family's influence within the labor sector. However, despite having the easy way in, his involvement in the family's illicit activities came with a fair share of challenges.

In 1976, Big Joe was accused of being involved in an unsuccessful attempt to eliminate Faust Novino. The alleged hit was claimed to be set up by a long-time associate and friend of Novino, Louis Pisa. Louis had come to Novino and proposed that the two commit burglary at a warehouse on the west side of Buffalo. Novino was under the assumption that it was just him and Pisa in the location, but he quickly noticed a large, heavyset man raising his arm to hit him. The man was later identified as John Sacco, but in response to the attempted attack, Novino pulled out his pistol and shot the attacker. Sacco wasn't the only one there, as stated by Novino. He heard footsteps behind him; so, he turned around and fired in that direction. He shot the second attacker, who would be identified as long-time Todaro family figure Leonard Falzone. Faust then saw two men, who he recognized as Todaro Jr. and Frank Billiteri, crouched on either side of him. He felt boxed in, so he shot back at the two previous attackers again. Falzone was shot at again, and Sacco was back on the attack. Novino tried shooting at the approaching Sacco's chest, but his gun jammed. He then made a break for it, finding refuge behind a large rolled-up rug. Eventually, he was able to get out of the warehouse through a door that led out to the streets. This incident was a major turning point in Big Joe's life, as it highlighted the dangers and explosiveness of the criminal underworld. This was an important lesson at this time because the constant threat of violence hung heavy over the entirety of organized crime, and it would highlight the lengths some would go to protect themselves or to get ahead.

In 1984, Big Joe transcended the business manager position that gave him a solid front for other activities. The younger Todaro now had a position of significant power within the Buffalo Crime Family. This came, of course, after the retirement of Sam Frangiamore and the ascension of Papa Joe to head of the now-Todaro Family. Todaro Jr. would take his place as the underboss, which was the first time in the family's decades-long history that leadership positions were held within a bloodline.

Todaro Jr. was now seated comfortably as second-in-command to his father, which gave him a significant amount of influence over the family's operations. It also established his positioning for his eventual ascent to the role of boss, which would continue everything that his father put into place while navigating the organization through a new era.

The Buffalo Crime Family and the 1990s

The landscape of organized crime was changing, and while it was difficult for Papa Joe to navigate that landscape as a boss, it was equally difficult for his underboss. Much of what happened during this period also involved Papa Joe, so this will review some of that with a focus on Todaro Jr.

Let's revisit 1989: This was when the FBI filed its statement in connection with a gambling investigation. They had identified both Todaro Sr. and Todaro Jr. leaders of the Buffalo Crime Family. Federal agents stated that the father-son duo was in charge of various underworld rackets. Their statements to the courts also mentioned that Todaro Jr. had more power at this time and that Todaro Sr. was semi-retired and splitting his time between his properties in Florida and New York.

In addition to Big Joe being identified as the de facto leader, those statements also identified Leonard Falzone as running loansharking operations and Victor and Daniel Sansanese as runners of a bookmaking operation for the Todaro Family. All of this information stemmed from when the FBI wiretapped Falzone's union-owned car to link the family to an illegal gambling case. While there were a few key statements made, the bug in Falzone's car failed to give any solid evidence to link the Todaros to the case.

In 1990, Todaro Jr. gave up his position as a business agent of the Laborers' International Union of North America after more investigations were done to uncover Local 210's ties to organized crime. Big Joe's resignation from the organization marked a huge turning point in his long career, as it highlighted the tremendous challenges that he faced because of his involvement in the crime family's operations.

In 1996, the Todaros were on the receiving end of scrutiny once again. The two were identified among 24 alleged figures in organized crime. Again, this was the group accused of influencing the Laborers' International Union of North America since the 1960s. While not much came from these accusations, it still underscored that the Buffalo Crime Family had long been tied to labor racketeering, which had been a very lucrative operation for the Mafia.

In 1999, Todaro Jr. along with Papa Joe and 16 others faced a civil racketeering lawsuit for their control of Local 210 through different acts of racketeering over the years. This all stemmed from the testimony of Ronald Fino, who was a former business manager of Local 210 and, again, a later informant for the FBI. The complaint filed in court identified Big Joe as the underboss of the Buffalo crime family. The father and son were also named as the owners of La Nova Pizzeria and Todaro's time serving as Local 210's business manager before resigning in 1990 was also brought up. This was important because although Todaro had resigned from that position, he still tried to maintain control over Local 210 with the help of Peter Gerace and Peter Capitano. These associates of Todaro's held positions in Local 210.

Todaro Sr.'s Retirement And Rumors

Joseph "Papa Joe" Todaro Sr., the well-tenured patriarch of the Todaro Crime Family, retired in 2006. There was now a scramble in law enforcement, as they were trying to identify the person that took over the role of the boss. The initial assumption was that Leonard Falzone had taken Todaro Sr.'s spot; however, others thought Falzone was simply acting as a "front boss" for the Todaro family. This was just an acting boss role that would let Big Joe transition into the role of leader for the family.

The FBI had charts of the Buffalo Crime Family's hierarchy, which lasted until Todaro Sr.'s retirement in 2006. These charts gave a look into the family's structure. This is how they came to the assumption that Falzone had taken over the top position of the family. However, when Papa Joe died in 2012, followed by the death of Ben "Sonny" Nicoletti in 2013, new rumors arose about the family's leadership.

These new speculations especially rose in 2012 when Matt Gryta (a crime reporter for The Buffalo News) claimed that the Buffalo family had spread its operations across the nation through telemarketing schemes, "pump-and-dump" stock market scams, and even internet pornography. While there wasn't much proof there to confirm Gryta's claims, it did highlight that the world of organized crime was changing with the times and making a significant shift away from the operations they had used before.

Another article came out that same year from Dan Herbeck. His article was about Ronald Fino, titled "Life After Local 210 for the FBI's Inside Guy" highlighted how Fino remained skeptical about claims from the US Justice Department that mob influences had been completely purged from not just Local 210 but the entirety of the Laborers' International Union of North America. Fino told Herbeck that while he believed that the government's initiative to clean up the unions had been a good start, they had not gone deep enough to really be free of Mafia control.

Those wouldn't be the only rumors launched against the Todaro Family. In 2013, The Toronto Star's organized crime reporter, Peter Edwards, made his claims that the family was trying to recover from their most recent downside by running loansharking operations out of the Casino Niagara in Canada. There was more than enough room to speculate. Had the family remained as resilient as they had been since the early 1900s? Were these articles just stabs in the dark? Even in the age of information, there was still so much uncertainty.

During the late 2000s, some news did come out about a homeowner association having ties to the Todaro family. A witness had come forward to the FBI, claiming that a company called Silver Lining Construction was involved in the scam and was part of the New York Mob. There was some weight to this claim though, as the company's owner, Leon Benzer, had a close association with attorney John Spilotro, who was the nephew of Vegas Mafia member Tony Spilotro. Those claims would progress after investigators disclosed the name of one of the key players in the homeowner association takeovers. They identified Paul Citelli who had already been known to have ties to the Buffalo Mob. Joseph Bravo, another defendant in the homeowner association scam, would be indicted with Citelli for their involvement in a cocaine trafficking ring run during the first decade of Todaro Sr.'s leadership. It would be during this period that the Buffalo mob was considered *the* family in control of the streets of Las Vegas.

The Canadian Connection

Nearly two decades after the Lee Coppola article, "The Withered Arm," in March 2017, Dan Herbeck—author of "Life After Local 210 for the FBI's Inside Guy"—penned a similar article to Coppola's called, "The Mafia is All But Dead in Western New York." By Herbeck's account, the FBI field office in Buffalo had said the once-powerful Buffalo Crime Family had become nothing more than scattered remnants. The article also claimed that those scatterings were either no longer active or lacked any real organization. It was a piece that strongly mirrored the 1998 Coppola article, with all the information leading to the conclusion that the Buffalo family had declined into a powerless organization.

However, much like Coppola's article, the events that took place following that report would say that doomsaying the Buffalo Crime Family was premature. In November of that year, there were a series of arrests made by the Royal Canadian Mounted Police. These were done in an operation known as Project OTremens, which negated yet another article. The family was still very active, and the evidence was backed up by FBI reports and Canadian newspapers.

Among those arrested during Project OTremens were Giuseppe (Joe) and Domenico Violi, both of whom had ties to the Buffalo family for years. The Violis were charged with trafficking narcotics, which hinted at the fact that the longstanding mafia drug trafficking ring that went from Ontario to Buffalo and Montreal to New York City was still very much alive. This was the same ring that had been established by The Undertaker, Stefano Magaddino, and Magaddino's cousin, Joseph Bonanno.

Michael McGarrity from the FBI said the operation had uncovered the roots of the decades-old partnership that formed the trafficking triangle. This revelation also showed that organized crime had evolved significantly from the days of neighborhood gangs and prominent figures. Things were moving back in the shadows and spreading across many figures, making it harder to track.

Peter Edwards, who was a seasoned journalist for the Toronto Star, would have another report come out in September 2018, which would make the proclamation that the Buffalo Crime Family was far from over, which had been the opposite of many of his contemporaries and other media reports. This explosive article claimed that the Todaro Family still had more than enough power to influence a recent mob war that was happening between several crime families in the Hamilton, Ontario, underworld.

Giving credit to Edwards' article were his sources, which included Paul Manning, a former undercover police officer in Hamilton, whose specialty was working on organized crime investigations. Manning was unsure of who would be standing tall after the dust settled from the war, but he was certain that the Buffalo family would always have the final word on the matter. It was this explosive statement that underscored the everlasting influence of the Buffalo mob and its Canadian connections that were established during the DiCarlo days and solidified during the reign of Magaddino.

That same article by Edwards would also go to state that the Todaro family had to give their approval for any high-level killings. This meant that any significant hits in the Canadian crime families had to go through Todaro and his underbosses. More of Edwards' sources stated that the leaders in Buffalo, at one point during the

Canadian family dispute, turned their backs on one side of it and gave its approval to the other. While both sides of the feuding Ontario organizations were supposed to be under Buffalo's control, they only controlled aspects of the business, which underscored that their chosen side in the dispute was likely the one getting the least number of kickbacks for themselves.

In the same month that the Edwards article came out, Al Iavarone of Ancaster, Ontario, was murdered as an act of retaliation for the murder of Angelo Musitano, which had taken place in May 2017. It would be Angelo's hit though that spawned the most speculation. While revenge was one of the reasons given for Angelo's death, rumors began to circulate that the hit was ordered in relation to unpaid debts and rivalries between Mafia members in the Niagara region, along with the influence of the Todaro family. There was even further speculation that the hit didn't just come down from the Buffalo family but that it came from Domenico Violi, who hadn't yet been revealed as an underboss in the Todaro family. Violi was one of those arrested after the investigation into the drug trafficking ring but had since found his place of influence in the Buffalo family. An interesting aspect of this hit was that Angelo's murder happened 20 years to the month after Musitano hitman Kenneth Murdock killed Johnny Papalia, the long-time captain of the Buffalo family (and head of the Papalia Crime Family), and Carman Barillaro (soldier for both the Buffalo and Papalia families).

The news would continue to roll out from Canada, as the Toronto Sun would go on to claim that the mob war in Southern Ontario was rooted in a decades-old conflict that had eventually led to the murder of Paolo Violi, along with his brothers Francesco and

Rocco, in Montreal during the late 1970s. The claim also named the Rizzuto family as the ones who ordered the hit. It was largely a theory, but it was suggested that there was a power struggle that was overwhelming the Rizzuto family. Their biggest threat was the Calabrese family, which had a large base set up in Toronto while also being a big player in New York. The growth of the Calabreses after being pushed aside by the Rizzutos fueled the war between the Buffalo-controlled Canadian factions.

On December 3, 2018, Domenico Violi received an eight-year prison sentence for his involvement in the drug trafficking ring that Project OTremens had exposed. During an investigation as part of the project, police wiretapped conversations between a law enforcement agent and Dom Violi were released. These conversations revealed discussions about a variety of activities and other opportunities. Violi was exposed for trafficking large amounts of drugs, ranging from PCP and MDMA to meth. Furthermore, those drugs were moved to an undercover RCMP agent in exchange for nearly $500,000, with over $20,000 in profit for Violi.

Those same wiretaps also confirmed that Violi had been appointed in October 2017 as an underboss of the Todaro Family by the main boss Joseph Todaro Jr. during a meeting in Florida. This made Violi the first Canadian mafioso to hold the second-highest position in the American Mafia. Dom (through the wiretap revelations) was heard bragging that he had beaten out 30 other people for the title of underboss. This was damning, as it revealed that the Buffalo family had, at minimum, 30 made men. These made men included members like Violi's uncles Natale and Rocco Luppino.

In his new elevated role, Violi was expected to take over control of the operations of the Luppino-Violi crime family and further establish his power base. The expectation was also to do this through further and greater collaboration with the Mafia families based in New York. The wiretaps also revealed what The Commission had been up to. This was because Violi's promotion was unusual enough that Big Joe had to consult with the Mafia's governing body for permission to promote Violi as an underboss for the Buffalo family.

Current Standings of the Todaro Family

In the opening months of 2019, another significant event occurred in the world of organized crime, and it was one that directly affected the Todaro Family. Cece Luppino, the son of Rocco Luppino and grandson of Giacomo Luppino, was killed tragically at the Luppino family home in Hamilton, Ontario.

The wiretap evidence from the case built around the Violi brothers revealed that Giuseppe Violi had told an undercover agent back in 2015 that Cece was under consideration to be inducted as a "made" man. There were problems though, as Cece would express concern to his father that he would only be involved in the family if it was profitable. In short, he was concerned that there were too many problems throughout the family, which was not something that would have been pleasing to hear from the rest of the Todaro organization. In the wake of Cece Luppino's murder, the Hamilton Police would take the search for his killer across the Canadian border into US territory. Canadian agents requested that law enforcement and news outlets in the Buffalo area show the images of their suspect that were captured by surveillance cameras.

Another hit was ordered in April 2019 when an attempt was made on Pasquale "Pat" Musitano's life while he was outside of Joseph Irving's (Musitano's lawyer) office. The investigation of the attempt showed that Pat was shot four times—once in the head. The Buffalo News brought to light that Musitano had enemies in mafioso circles in Montreal and Buffalo. Once again, it would be Peter Edwards who asserted that he was more convinced at this point that the Buffalo Crime Family was involved in the shooting. This came after a source had made mention of the organization at the same time as talking about the shooting.

That claim by Edwards would be strengthened after a CBC News report came out of Canada, which stated that Domenico Violi was recorded in September 2017, saying that the murder of Angelo Musitano was committed to send a very clear message to Angelo's brother. Violi also told the same informant that Pat would be next, and he would be dead before the holidays, which would get rid of one more of the family's "headaches." The headache for the family would be gone by mid-2020. In July of that year, Pat Musitano would meet his gruesome end when he was shot and killed in Burlington.

In 2020, which proved to be a quiet year for most of the world mired in a pandemic, things were still changing for the Todaro family. Longtime member Frank BiFulco passed away, leaving a significant hole in the organization. Another revelation that year came when the FBI and the RCMP put out a report that Albert Iavarone's murder in September 2018 was in association with the ongoing turf war in Hamilton, Ontario. Their joint report also connected Iavarone to the bosses of the Musitano family. The investigation conducted by both agencies showed that the bosses from the New York families had gotten together with Tommy Gambino (boss in Los Angeles) to induct Iavarone into the L.A. family. It was the New York families that wanted the inductee to be a liaison between the US and Ontario groups, but it was a move that had angered several members of the Todaro family, who were the overseers of underworld activity in the areas of Western New York and Southern Ontario.

The most recent news about the Buffalo Crime Family was that Domenico Violi had been granted day parole, which set rumors in motion that there was a significant development in the Todaro Family's future.

CHAPTER 9

THE CURRENT REGIME AND THE FUTURE OF ORGANIZED CRIME

As seen in the most recent years of the Todaro family, information is all but murky. Reporters make conflicting articles; in some, the family is alive and well, and in others, the family is dead and buried. There's even conflicting information about Big Joe. He denies any role or leadership position in the crime family, yet evidence still surfaces about activity that ties back to Buffalo. This chapter serves as a look at the current (alleged) hierarchy of the Buffalo Crime Family, and it will also provide a glimpse into what the future may hold for Buffalo and the American Mafia as a whole. Is the once-notorious underworld of America gone? Or have they mastered the art of blending into the shadows once again as they once did?

Administrators

Boss: Joseph A. "Big Joe" Todaro Jr.

Again, while Big Joe has said that he is not a part of the world of organized crime, things have been linked back to him since he took power in the mid-2000s. The Todaro name is one that still commands respect in the region and organized crime. While following in his father's footsteps with Mafia activities, he also took ownership of the La Nova Pizzeria in Buffalo, a legitimate, lucrative business in the area. Big Joe's journey to the top of the mountain wasn't easy, but it was marked with plenty of determination and resilience.

To recap, in the mid-1980s, Joseph Todaro Sr. claimed the top position of the Buffalo family, finally providing stability after the passing of Stefano Magaddino in 1974. He recognized his son's potential and promoted him to the position of Underboss. This was a significant move, not just for Big Joe but the entirety of the Buffalo organization.

Nearly a decade after becoming an underboss, Todaro Jr. along with Leonard Falzone, Frank BiFulco, and John and Joseph Pieri were forcefully removed from Local 210. It was a setback because labor racketeering was still lucrative, but it wouldn't deter Big Joe.

Finally, when Papa Joe Todaro retired in 2006, Big Joe would take over for his father, marking the first time the Buffalo family's head position was passed to a blood relative. His underboss would be longtime Buffalo member Leonard Falzone, and Falzone would keep that role until 2016 when he passed away. Around a year later, in a unique move for the Buffalo outfit, Big Joe made Canadian mafioso Domenico Violi his underboss. It was a strategic move for the family, and it needed the approval of the Mafia since Violi was Canadian.

Underboss: Domenico "Dom" Violi

Domenico Violi is the first underboss of the Buffalo family who operates from a Canadian faction. His journey to the top is one of tenacity and resilience, and it underscores why Todaro Jr. would choose him for the position.

His grandfather was Giacomo Luppino who was the boss of the Luppino Crime Family in Hamilton, Ontario. Dom's father, Paolo Violi, operated in the Cotroni family out of Montreal and served as a capo to the Bonanno crime family. However, Paolo's life was tragically cut short when he was murdered by a Sicilian faction of the Cotroni family. It would be this tragic event that would have the most impact on Dom, shaping the course of the rest of his life.

After Paolo's death, Domenico moved back to Hamilton with his mother and brother, Giuseppe "Joe" Violi. Joe Violi is also a member of the Luppino family. In January 2015, Domenico, after doing his share of work, became a made man in the Todaro Crime Family. It was a significant milestone in Domenico's journey, and it cemented his position in the world of organized crime.

In October 2017, over two years after becoming a made member of the Todaro family, Domenico met with Joeseph Todaro Jr. in Florida where Todaro promoted him to Underboss of the Todaro family. Again, this made Dom the first Canadian to hold the second-highest position in the American Mafia.

Domenico was arrested after a lengthy investigation, and he would be given eight years in prison after he pleaded guilty to drug trafficking charges. In November 2021 though, Dom was given day parole.

Consigliere: Unknown

This position in the Buffalo crime family is unknown at the moment. However, the consigliere is one of the key figures in a crime family, giving advice and guidance to both the boss and the underboss. Despite uncertainty about the position, someone is definitely still filling this role because it remains a crucial component of the family's structure and operations. The person in this position plays a huge part in shaping the family's future.

Caporegimes

Buffalo Faction

Like consigliere, the person currently serving as caporegime for Buffalo's operations is unknown. This move could be done intentionally to keep operations away from the eyes of the public and law enforcement.

Canadian Faction

On the Canadian side of things, Rocco Luppino fills the role of caporegime, leading the Luppino Crime Family in Hamilton, Ontario. Rocco comes from a long lineage of influential figures in the Mafia. His father was Giacomo Luppino, a powerful member of the Buffalo family who had a considerable amount of power and influence.

Rocco's brother, Natale "Nat" Luppino also serves on the crew as a soldier, which further strengthens the Luppinos' presence in the Buffalo Crime Family. But the Luppinos' have faced their share of tragedy too. The most recent tragedy was the brutal murder of Cece Luppino, Rocco's son, in front of Natale's home in Hamilton.

Soldiers

Buffalo Faction

Victor Sansanese

Victor Sansanese is a long-serving soldier in the Buffalo faction of the Todaro family. His lineage is also deeply intertwined in the fabric of organized crime. His father, Daniel G. Sansanese, and his brother, Daniel Sansanese Jr., have both dedicated their lives to the Buffalo family. Victor would follow suit, becoming a made man in the mid-1970s, which marked his official entrance into the family.

In 1989, both Victor and Daniel Sansanese Jr. were identified as officials in Local 210. Along with the identification came the accusations that the brothers were controlling bookmaking operations for the new Todaro family, which was one of their most significant operations at this time. However, things would end a few years later for Victor and Local 210 when he was removed from his position as a director of training. It was a pretty big shakeup that would send ripple effects throughout the Todaro family.

Robert "Bobby" Panaro

Bobby Panaro is a soldier for the Buffalo faction while stationed in Las Vegas, highlighting the reach of power the family still has in the criminal underworld. In Vegas, he runs a car dealership, which provides a legitimate front for any illegal activities. Panaro, as mentioned earlier, was indicted in 1997, along with members of the Los Angeles crime family, for murdering and robbing Herbert Blitzstein, who had been a Las Vegas associate of the Chicago organization. This was another event that caused a major ripple effect in the criminal underworld, especially in the Todaro family.

John A. Pieri

John Pieri was made to fill the role of soldier. His father, Joseph Pieri, and his uncle, Sam Pieri, were both high-ranking members of the family. In 1996, Pieri along with his brother Joseph Pieri Jr, Big Joe, Leonard Falzone, and Frank BiFulco were all pushed out of Local 210, seemingly ending the family's control over the operation.

Peter Gerace Sr.

Peter is a soldier with a high-ranking connection in the Buffalo family. His father-in-law was Joseph Todaro Sr., which made his brother-in-law Joseph Todaro Jr. Both of Gerace's sons, Peter Jr. and Anthony, serve as associates to the family as well. Before Gerace and other members of the Buffalo family were removed from Local 210, he had served as the union's president, business manager, and business agent. He would continue to hold his business manager position until he stepped down later on.

Donald "The Turtle" Panepinto

Donald is another soldier in the Buffalo family and a former member of Local 210 who has years of service under his belt. Donald's sons, Marc and Don, were both members of 210 and would go on to become lawyers. Donald's ties to the Buffalo Crime Family were cemented on September 6, 1993, when his daughter (Dana Christine Panepinto) married Joseph Todaro III, the son of future family boss Big Joe Todaro.

Things were quiet for Panepinto for a couple of years after the removal from Local 210 until in March 2000 when Donald and several other figures were indicted and charged with the illegal operation of a gambling business, which he had been running out of the Donato Social Club.

In 2014, Donald's oldest son, Marc, would win a seat on the New York State Senate, a position he only held until 2017. Marc would then plead guilty in 2018 to federal corruption charges that stemmed from unwanted advances on a Senate staff member. Marc would get two months in prison and lose his ability to practice law for a year.

Canadian Faction

Natale "Nat" Luppino

As mentioned before, Natale is a Luppino crew soldier operating in the Hamilton area. He is the son of the powerful Canadian Mafia member Giacomo Luppino, and his brother Rocco serves as a capo of the crew.

Giuseppe "Joe" Violi

Joe also operates out of Hamilton and has deep ties with the Mafia. His father was a capo for the Bonnano family's faction that was in Montreal. His ties are further cemented in the mafia through his brother, Domenico, who is the underboss of the Todaro family.

Associates

Buffalo Faction

Joseph Edward "Joey" Todaro III

Joey is Big Joe's son, which means that the youngest Todaro is a prominent figure in the Buffalo Crime Family. His lineage places him in a very precarious position to follow in his father's footsteps as the Mafia pushes forward into the future.

In October 1989, Joey was indicted for felony assault when he beat William Gorman with a baseball bat. Gorman had been a bouncer at Celebrities Nite Club in the Cheektowaga Ramada Renaissance Hotel, and the beating was certainly a blemish on the already-struggling family.

In June 1993, Joey Todaro, Frank BiFulco, Gaetano Miceli, John Catanzaro, Frank Tripi, Samuel Amoia Jr. (Sam Pieri's grandson), Michael A Muscarella, Larry Panaro, Steve Sacco, and Vincent Spano were all identified in their involvement in a telemarketing scam raided by the FBI.

Much like Big Joe, Joey Todaro III runs an offshoot location of La Nova Pizzeria. While this has come under scrutiny for both father and son, the business is legitimate and provides them with a large amount of credibility.

Peter "Pete" Gerace Jr. and Anthony Gerace

Pete runs Pharaoh's Gentleman's Club in Cheektowaga, which is owned by his father. Since Peter Sr. is married to Big Joe Todaro's sister, the Club has close ties (and likely acts as a front) for the underworld activities of the Buffalo Crime Family. Peter's brother Anthony is also a soldier, making the Gerace family a powerful force for the Todaro family.

In 2000, Gerace and Michael Geiger were indicted on one count each of wire fraud for their involvement in a telemarketing scheme. From around late 1992 until February 1995, the men would claim they worked for Advanced Distributing Company. Their setup was promising their victims that they could win a new car or large sums of money. Gerace eventually pleaded guilty to everything in 2005, after the hearings were delayed over a dispute about admissible evidence.

On December 17, 2019, Gerace's strip club was raided by Homeland Security following the indictment of Anthony and retired Buffalo DEA agent Joe Bongiovanni on drugs and weapons charges.

Peter Capitano Jr. and Sam Capitano

Peter and Sam are notable associates of the Buffalo family, as they are part of the Pizza Gang. The Capitanos were identified by undercover operative Ron Fino as being strong associates of both Victor Sansanese and Big Joe Todaro.

In 1996, the brothers would lead an opposing faction that would fight back against the federal trusteeship of Local 210. The trusteeship was to be put into place with the intention of getting rid of mob control and influence in the unions, and it would be the Capitanos' resistance that would lead to them being suspended for one year, with neither being able to hold a leadership role for the next five years.

Sam, in particular, let his fiery temper flare during the meetings. In one of these heated debates, he verbally attacked Gabe Rosetti, and on the next day, the two were involved in a fistfight. That fight would lead to Rosetti firing Sam Capitano from the board, which Sam would contest before the National Labor Relations Board.

Michael Masecchia

Masecchia is an associate of the Buffalo family and has a storied past with authority. In August 2019, the FBI and Homeland Security searched his home as part of an ongoing investigation into organized crime and public corruption. The agents uncovered homemade explosives, stolen firearms, and narcotics, but that would just be the beginning. A criminal complaint had also been made against Masecchia, which identified him as a drug dealer who had a long 20-year history of growing and distributing tremendous amounts of marijuana.

In September 2020, a grand jury indictment would name the associate as a part of Italian Organized Crime, and they would make note that law enforcement had already labeled him as such or possibly a made member of the Buffalo family. The heart of the indictment lies in the allegation that Michael Masecchia bribed then-DEA agent Joseph Bongiovanni to stop any investigations into himself and any others that were suspected of being associated with the local Mafia. The bribe worked because despite being investigated several times by the DEA between 2008 and 2019, Masecchia was never arrested or charged with any crimes while Bongiovanni was part of the DEA.

Michael also has more ties to the Buffalo family. He is married to Krista Mazzara, whose father Bart was alleged by prosecutors to be a made man in Buffalo. Krista also has ties to the Mafia, as her uncles are Dan and Victor Sansanese.

Utica Faction

Russell E. "Russ" Carcone

Russ is one of the most notable members of the Buffalo family that operates within the Utica region. Russ's journey to his position was a long one, starting in 1989 when Carcone, his father Benedetto, and several others were indicted on racketeering charges. This was a significant escalation in the Utica faction's conflict with the law, as it highlighted just how deeply they were tied to the criminal underworld.

In December 1990, Russ, Benedetto, Jack Minicone Jr., Anthony Inserra, and Jack Zogby were all convicted of running a criminal enterprise centered in Utica. This enterprise operated for nearly 20 years (1973 to 1989), and they were involved in multiple activities like extortion, loansharking, illegal gambling, the trafficking of stolen property, and murder. Backing this up was Benny's, Russ's father's, involvement. Benny ran the Swap Shop in Utica and used a large portion of his influence over local bookies, forcing them to make large, regular payments to him and his son.

In 2000, another indictment was brought down on 25 individuals for being involved in a Utica-based shoplifting and fencing ring. The group would steal items from various retail store chains like Walmart, K-Mart, CVS, and other stores around Oneida, Herkimer, Fulton, Madison, Montgomery, Albany, and various other counties in upstate New York. The shoplifting ring took a different approach. Instead of stealing and selling high-value items, they were focusing on items that would do quick resell like razors, batteries, and compact discs.

Russ lost his father in March 2004, and while Benny's death marked the end of an era for Utica, Russ was doing more than enough to carry the legacy. It's a role that he still fills today.

Allied Groups

Buffalo Chapter of the Outlaws

One of the Buffalo Crime Family's biggest allies is the Buffalo chapter of the Outlaws Motorcycle Club. Their connection in this alliance is through one John "Tommy O" Ermin, who coincidentally serves as the national president of the motorcycle club.

Before Ermin was promoted to this high-ranking position, he had served as president of the Buffalo chapter of the Outlaws, and during his time in that position, he established some strong ties with the Buffalo Mafia. He developed particularly strong ties to Joesph "Big Joe" Todaro Jr., and this connection between the two organizations played a huge role in strengthening their alliances while expanding both their influences.

In April 2021, Joseph Tripi (Assistant US Attorney) came out and revealed that Ermin, who was also holding a general manager position at Pharaoh's Gentleman's Club in Cheektowaga, had actually climbed higher and assumed the role of international president of the Outlaws. This was another significant milestone for all parties, as it reopened speculation about how far the Buffalo Crime Family's influence would reach.

Niagara Chapter of the Hells Angels (Canada)

Another notable ally for the Buffalo family is the Hells Angels Motorcycle Club in Canada. The president of the Canadian chapter is Gerald "Skinny" Ward, who started his association with the Buffalo organization in the late 1990s. His involvement started primarily with buying and distributing cocaine in the Hamilton,

Ontario area, which contributed to the illicit drug ring that had become a significant part of the Buffalo family's activities.

Ward's alliance with the Hells Angels actually sprung up around the same time in 1998, and he and his smaller outfit joined the motorcycle gang in 2000. By 2008, police estimated that Ward and the Niagara chapter of the Hells Angels had nearly taken over the entire cocaine racket in the region. Not only did this underscore the extent of the Hells Angels' involvement in the Todaro family's drug ring, but it also showed that the Angels were just as big a part of the family as the family members themselves.

When the national president of Hells Angels Canada, Walter "Nurget" Stadnick, was taken in by police in 2001, Ward stepped in to become a co-leader. It was a tremendous shift, and as seen with the estimation taken by police, it was also an effective shift. Ward cemented his place in the Hells Angels and became a valuable asset to the Buffalo Crime Family.

The Future of Organized Crime and the Buffalo Crime Family

What the future holds for the Buffalo family is uncertain. While they, and other Mafia outfits, have held on to some sort of power, the landscape of organized crime is evolving at an unprecedented rate. The traditional structures and operations that have shaped the Mafia since it began have had to undergo incredible changes, reshaped by advancements in technology, globalization, and increased efforts from law enforcement.

Future Activities

We are rapidly moving into the digital age, which means the face of organized crime is evolving even faster and becoming even more sophisticated. Cybercrimes, for example, have seen a significant surge in recent years. These activities span a wide range of illegal operations including identity theft, online fraud, hacking and phishing schemes, and many others. Criminal organizations have found how to exploit the anonymity given to them by the internet, which allows them to carry these activities out with little risk of detection.

Then there is also the dark web, a hidden part of the internet that can only be accessed with specific software, which has long been a hotbed for illegal activities. It gives a platform for organized crime syndicates to do their business in a way that they have long been accustomed to—far from the sight and reach of law enforcement. From drug trafficking to arms deals, the dark web has become rife with all sorts of illegal goods and services.

In particular, human trafficking and modern slavery have emerged as areas of high concern for authorities across the world. These awful crimes are highly lucrative, making them attractive to any organization looking to maximize revenue. Organizations look to lure vulnerable people under pretenses and then exploit them, and many times those individuals disappear without a trace.

However, before we get into more details in the next section, we should note that while organized crime has found new avenues, thanks to technology, so has law enforcement. Law enforcement agencies across the globe are using the same resources to analyze data, find patterns, and stop criminal activity before it happens.

Law Enforcement Crackdown

The landscape of organized crime as we know it is changing rapidly. As criminal networks become more sophisticated and globalized, law enforcement agencies around the world are also stepping up their efforts to combat the growing threats. Authorities are investing in new technologies and tools, and they are making a shift toward international cooperation as they move away from traditional investigative strategies.

One of the most significant developments in their efforts is the use of artificial intelligence (AI) and machine learning in investigations. These technologies have changed the way these agencies operate. AI and machine learning algorithms can sift through vast amounts of data in a short amount of time, identifying patterns and connections that can easily get past human investigators. This is particularly helpful in cases involving organized crime, where criminal networks make the extra effort to keep their activities hidden. AI and machine learning will analyze everything, including financial records, phone records, surveillance footage, and even social media activity. Investigators will take those findings and piece together the intricate web of activity, leading them to more accurate conclusions.

Moreover, algorithms can be trained to identify specific types of activity, which allows law enforcement to identify specific threats from these networks. For example, machine learning algorithms can be trained to find behavior patterns associated with money laundering or human trafficking, which lets law enforcement take proactive measures.

However, the use of these tools comes with its own set of challenges. A large amount of data is needed for these tools to function effectively, and collecting this amount of data starts to raise concerns over privacy. Also, AI and machine learning are only as good as the data that they are trained on, so biases in data can lead to biases in results, which can lead to inaccuracies. Therefore, there has to be a greater level of care to ensure that these tools are used responsibly, ensuring that agencies aren't infringing on individual rights or creating biased algorithms that highlight existing inequality.

While they are using new technologies, law enforcement agencies have also discovered that international cooperation is just as important to combat organized crime. As these organizations become increasingly globalized, crimes spread to multiple jurisdictions, making it harder for one specific agency to fight them alone. To overcome that challenge, agencies now band together more than ever before, sharing intelligence and resources to go after these threats. This can come in various forms, from taking part in joint investigations and operations to exchanging agents and other resources. International organizations like Interpol also play a key role in ensuring this cooperation.

As criminal networks continue to evolve, the strategies used to fight them have to evolve too. When agencies can embrace new technologies and work together with other agencies, they can hope to keep pace with the criminal underworld's activities.

The Buffalo Crime Family

The Buffalo Crime Family, like any other organized crime outfit, isn't immune to these changing times. The family has shown a huge knack for adapting and evolving over the years, from the early days when Palmeri founded the family to its modern incarnation as the Todaro Crime Family under Big Joe Todaro. The organization has always navigated the changing landscape with resilience, and it has continued to exude just as much power and influence as it did before.

Looking ahead, and this is merely speculation based on what we've seen from the family in the last century, the Buffalo Crime Family will most likely continue to evolve and stay ahead of the curve in response to the changing dynamics. For example, they will see the rise of cybercrime as a threat and an opportunity. Increased activity online does open the door for law enforcement to track their activity, but it also lets the family find new opportunities to expand what they are doing and increase profits.

The increased efforts by law enforcement also pose a significant challenge for the family. As seen throughout this book, there has always been a great deal of invisibility and anonymity to their work. Even if the authorities have ever learned more than the public, it hasn't been much, at least based on the information that exists. However, with law enforcement's investments in new technologies and ramped-up efforts to crack down on the world of organized crime, the Buffalo family will find it far more difficult to keep their normal level of invisibility.

So, while the future of organized crime and the Buffalo Crime Family is uncertain, what we do know is that things are rapidly changing, and the criminal underworld has made tremendous strides to stay ahead of the changes. They are becoming more sophisticated and globalized, which makes them much harder to track, at least for just one law enforcement agency. As time passes by, their ability to adapt to changes will determine their survival. That said, if anyone can navigate these changes, it's the Buffalo organization. Only time will tell though if the saga continues.

CONCLUSION

As we reach the end of this book, we leave behind a world that is still just as fascinating as it is terrifying. This small piece of the world, known as the Buffalo Crime Family, as you now know, is one of power and ambition, much like the Mafia counterparts you are more familiar with.

In this book, we have met men of tremendous power and ambition, who have risen from a place of obscurity to rule an empire. We saw how they navigated the treacherous landscape of the criminal underworld, forged alliances, and eliminated enemies as they pursued power and respect. We have witnessed their rise and fall—their victories and defeats.

Take a moment to consider that amidst some of these stories of power and ambition lies a deeper narrative. At the heart of it all is the human condition that speaks of every person's capacity for good and evil and how the choices we make and the paths we choose all matter in the grand scheme of things. While learning interesting facts about mobsters, you also get to confront the darker parts of human nature and truly look at your own values and beliefs. Think about how thin the line between right and wrong is and how one decision you make can change the entire course of your life.

Curious, no doubt, but even as you place the Buffalo family pin into your timeline, you'll see that once you start looking at the entirety of the Mafia, the idea that a lot of these figures and families likely made their own history because of one crucial choice suddenly makes complete sense.

REFERENCES

Bruno, A. (n.d.). *The Banana War — Joe Bonanno: A man of honor. A crime family epic.* Crimelibrary.org. https://crimelibrary.org/gangsters_outlaws/family_epics/bonanno/3.html

Buffalo police then and now - Mob boss Stefano Magaddino cheats death, twice. (n.d.). Www.bpdthenandnow.com. https://www.bpdthenandnow.com/bombing1936.html

Cascio, J. (2022, November 1). *Apalachin, NY: 14 November 1957.* Mafia Genealogy. https://mafiagenealogy.com/2022/11/01/apalachin-ny-14-november-1957/

Daniele, G. (2023, January 27). *Modern mafia: Italy's organised crime machine has changed beyond recognition in 30 years.* The Conversation. https://theconversation.com/modern-mafia-italys-organised-crime-machine-has-changed-beyond-recognition-in-30-years-198352

Dickson, M. (2020, June 1). *Stefano "The Undertaker" Magaddino.* American Mafia History. https://americanmafiahistory.com/stefano-the-undertaker-magaddino/

Doyle, B. (2020, October 5). *The story of Willie Moretti — One of NJ's most infamous mobsters*. New Jersey 101.5. https://nj1015.com/the-story-of-willie-moretti-one-of-njs-most-infamous-mobsters/

Giuffrida, A. (2019, October 30). Italy mafia networks are more complex and powerful, says minister. *The Guardian*. https://www.theguardian.com/world/2019/oct/30/italy-mafia-networks-are-more-complex-and-powerful-says-minister

History.com Editors. (2019, June 7). *Mafia in the United States*. HISTORY; A&E Television Networks. https://www.history.com/topics/crime/mafia-in-the-united-states

Hunt, T. P., & Tona, M. A. (n.d.-a). *1921 confession revealed Good Killers gang*. Mafiahistory.us. https://mafiahistory.us/a014/f_goodkillers.html

Hunt, T. P., & Tona, M. A. (n.d.-b). *DiCarlo: Buffalo's first family of crime: Angelo Palmeri*. DiCarlo. https://buffalomob.blogspot.com/2013/10/angelo-palmeri-jan-12-1878-to-dec-21.html

Hunt, T. P., & Tona, M. A. (n.d.-c). *DiCarlo: Buffalo's first family of crime: Stefano Magaddino*. Buffalomob.blogspot.com. https://buffalomob.blogspot.com/search?q=stefano+magaddino

Hunt, T. P., & Tona, M. A. (n.d.-d). *Partial timeline of events in the book*. Buffalomob.com. https://buffalomob.com/p-tmline.html

Knight, M. (2021, April 17). *The commission trial lifted the lid on the New York mafia*. The Mob Museum. https://themobmuseum.org/blog/the-commission-trial-lifted-the-lid-on-the-new-york-mafia/

Margaritoff, M. (2022, October 24). *He led A mafia family for 35 years, then wrote a tell-all book about it — and somehow lived to tell the tale.* All That's Interesting.
https://allthatsinteresting.com/joe-bonanno

Marker, M. D. (2019). *Organized crime has gone high tech.* Policechiefmagazine.org.
https://www.policechiefmagazine.org/organized-crime-has-gone-high-tech/

Musariri, D. (2018, August 9). *Rise of the cyber mafia: How organised crime went digital.* NS Business. https://www.ns-businesshub.com/technology/cyber-mafia-organised-crime-digital/

NCS. (2012, December 17). *What was the Castellammarese War?* National Crime Syndicate; National Crime Syndicate.
https://www.nationalcrimesyndicate.com/castellammarese-war/

Peters, J. (2013, November 14). *On this day in 1957, the FBI finally had to admit that the Mafia existed.* Slate. https://slate.com/news-and-politics/2013/11/apalachin-meeting-on-this-day-in-1957-the-fbi-finally-had-to-admit-that-the-mafia-existed.html

Santolo, D. (2017, November 22). *Investigation spurs debate over Buffalo Mafia Family.* About the Mafia.
https://aboutthemafia.com/investigation-spurs-renewed-debate-over-the-status-of-the-buffalo-mafia-family/

Staff. (2013, February 24). *"Mafia Summit" explores how Magaddino's bad call did in the mob.* Buffalo News.
https://buffalonews.com/news/mafia-summit-explores-how-

magaddino-s-bad-call-did-in-the-mob/article_3a19cf89-76e0-5cab-8323-75c77d9495c1.html

The Week Staff. (2019, April 21). *The mafia today*. The Week. https://theweek.com/articles/835970/mafia-today

Wikipedia Contributors. (n.d.-a). *Apalachin meeting*. Wikipedia. https://en.wikipedia.org/wiki/Apalachin_meeting

Wikipedia Contributors. (n.d.-b). *Buffalo crime family*. Wikipedia. https://en.wikipedia.org/wiki/Buffalo_crime_family#Early_origins

Wikipedia Contributors. (n.d.-c). *Castellammarese War*. Wikipedia. https://en.wikipedia.org/wiki/Castellammarese_War

Wikipedia Contributors. (n.d.-d). *Joseph Todaro Sr.* Wikipedia. https://en.wikipedia.org/wiki/Joseph_Todaro_Sr.

Wikipedia Contributors. (n.d.-e). *Stefano Magaddino*. Wikipedia. https://en.wikipedia.org/wiki/Stefano_Magaddino

Wikipedia Contributors. (n.d.-f). *The Commission (American Mafia)*. Wikipedia. https://en.wikipedia.org/wiki/The_Commission_(American_Mafia)

Wikipedia Contributors. (n.d.-g). *War on drugs*. Wikipedia. https://en.wikipedia.org/wiki/War_on_Drugs

www.ingramcontent.com/pod-product-compliance
Lightning Source LLC
Chambersburg PA
CBHW050208130526
44590CB00043B/3219